D0742946

THE SPIRAL CALENDAR
AND ITS EFFECT ON
FINANCIAL MARKETS AND HUMAN EVENTS

WRITTEN & ILLUSTRATED
BY
CHRISTOPHER CAROLAN

NEW CLASSICS LIBRARY

The Spiral Calendar
and its Effect on Financial Markets and Human Events

© 1992 by Christopher L. Carolan.

All rights reserved.
No part of this book may be used or reproduced in any manner whatsoever without written permission except in the case of brief quotations embodied in critical articles or reviews. Violators will be prosecuted to the fullest extent of the law.

Design, layout, dustjacket artwork, Figures 3-6 and 3-9 photography and all illustrations except Figure 3-7 by Christopher Carolan.

Printed in the United States of America by Braun-Brumfield, Inc.

First Edition: October 1992
Second Printing: February 1993

For information address the publishers:
New Classics Library
Post Office Box 1618
Gainesville Georgia 30503
U.S.A.
ISBN 0-932750-21-4

Spiral Calendar™ is a trademark of Calendar Research, Inc.

for Madeleine

ACKNOWLEDGMENTS

The exchange of ideas with fellow technical analysts is a vital resource to anyone attempting to break new ground. Special thanks go to Bob Prechter who has had unlimited patience in the roles of advisor, editor and publisher. Those whose assistance has been invaluable include Dave Allman, Pete DeSario, Hank Pruden and Dan Steinberg.

I gratefully appreciate the understanding and patience of my family. I didn't grasp the effect of this project on them until my then three year old daughter's school class was asked what their parents did. "My daddy *lives* in the basement," was her reply.

All charts with pre 20th century prices are constructed from data provided by *The Foundation for the Study of Cycles*, Irvine California. The intra-day bond chart on page 94 is courtesy of *Tudor Investment Co.* Figure 3-7 is from *Scientific American,* March 1969. The chart for London stocks in Figure 10-5 is courtesy of *Yelton Fiscal, Inc.*

TABLE OF CONTENTS

FOREWORD

On the evening of Wednesday, October 11, 1989, I met Christopher Carolan for the first time, at a dinner with four stock market professionals. The Dow Jones Industrial Average had hit a new all-time print high the previous day. Mr. Carolan was very emphatic about his new market timing discovery, which was based on a lunar calendar. "It calls for a sharp drop in the stock market, and we're out of time. It needs to happen right now." The next day, the Dow sold off 13 points. The following day, Friday, it began collapsing right from the opening bell, finally closing down 189 points, the third largest one-day percentage drop of the decade. Monday's down opening brought the Dow to a level almost 300 points below the high it had registered four trading days earlier. The juxtaposition of these events got my attention.

At about the same time, from 3000 miles away, a professional friend called to tell me what he had seen on television that night. One of the most popular astronomers in the U.S. was discussing a huge mural centuries old. It was absolutely remarkable, he said, that people way back then, without the aid of a telescope, had such a detailed, precise knowledge of the timing of the motions of the earth relative to the sun, moon and several planets. What keen observers they were! What lengthy records they must have kept! And how advanced scientifically and mathematically they had to have been! Then he pointed to an area of the mural that appeared to correlate the motions of the sun and moon with dramatic natural and human events. The astronomer dismissed this portion of the mural with a smirk and a wave of his hand. Belief in such correlation, he said, is of course superstitious nonsense.

Is that assertion true, or in fact contradictory to the evidence?

Let's examine the attitude of the astronomer. Scientists (including the one on television) and mathematicians probably constitute the largest block of humanity *least* likely to hold superstitious ideas. Since human nature, by all other evidence, has remained constant and reliable through the centuries, it seems unlikely that scientists of any prior age were highly superstitious. Just as scientists do today, they would have been the most likely people to ask, "Where is the evidence for this claim?" They would hardly be prone to marrying their intellectual achievements with detailed superstitious invention. The modern astronomer, then, was in fact presenting two contradictory ideas, first, that a group of people were consummate observers, detailed record keepers, and of scientific bent, and second, that these same people were asserting something that was obviously false, in fact silly. Moreover, the supposed false assertions could be supported or disproved precisely by observation and detailed record keeping, at which task they were proven experts. The knowledge of human events displayed on the mural reflected the same detailed record keeping as did the astronomic knowledge. Who, then, was actually being superstitious? The previous scientists, or the modern one who was certain, not merely without evidence, but contrary to character, that previously living scientists were as gullible as children?

Evidence that earlier record-keepers were onto something came in the 1970s, as climatologist Iben Browning, to the nearly universal condemnation of the geologic profession, published research indicating a correlation between peak tidal forces, as created by lunar and solar (actually Earth) cycles, and the occurrence of earthquakes and volcanoes. Indeed, as I write this page, the most powerful earthquake in southern California in forty years has just occurred, within hours of a volcano blowing off in Alaska. Although all commentary calls these events "unrelated," they are taking place 36 hours from a solar eclipse near a lunar perigee, during a year Dr. Browning described over a decade ago as being near the cyclic peak for such phenomena. Dr. Browning discovered not only this correlation, which helps forecast occurrences that are *themselves* often very dramatic events in human history, but found furthermore that major volcanic eruptions, because they cloud the atmosphere, are typically *followed* by a couple of years of cooler seasons (this year is already shaping up as one of the coolest of the past century), a shrinkage in food growing acreage, a resulting economic depression, social stress, and often classic human responses to such conditions, such as the breakup of political unions and war. In other words, he explained the mechanism for a direct link between lunar and solar cycles and a number of the human social experiences that provide drama in history.

Mr. Carolan's dramatic market call, Dr. Browning's work, plus the contradiction in the ideas held by the modern astronomer discussed above, appear to suggest an interesting idea, that some of our ancestors were more observant of the human condition than we are. Indeed, they may have discovered some valuable information about predicting the future that is being dismissed cavalierly by those who come across any such indication.

It is hardly a surprise that many pre-industrial cultures developed a keen interest in observing the motions in the solar system. Today, the availability and sophistication of nighttime electronic entertainment (while a blessing, to be sure), has reduced to near zero for most people the desire to observe the motions of Earth and moon every night. Centuries ago, the sky was probably the biggest attraction going, on a relative basis as bright and beckoning as Las Vegas or a video screen. Ultimately it became the equivalent of a giant detective game, as the participants tried to determine the outcome of its motions. How interesting that playing this intriguing game might also have led to the revelation of an even more startling fact, that the solutions bore a correlation to events in mankind's history. Rather than resulting from superstition, then, perhaps the ultimate intensity of our forefathers' interest in the sky was the result of a compelling new understanding, available only because of meticulous observation and detailed record keeping spanning centuries. Any mystical aura that may have attended such knowledge was probably due to the fact that there was no physically linking mechanism imaginable by ancient scientists.

The attainment of such an understanding may also account for the passion, dedication and effort behind the building of two of antiquity's greatest structures. The building of the Great Pyramid in Egypt was apparently undertaken and accomplished not only, as one author postulated, to serve as an astronomic observatory (a pool of still water around which astronomers apparently sat reflected a small "moving" patch of the sky that shone down a long straight shaft) but clearly also to preserve for millennia certain mathematical knowledge, including that of the golden, or Fibonacci, ratio. The linkage of these two purposes establishes the possibility that the Egyptians related astronomic events to other natural phenomena. The knowledge of the lunar-solar calendar had its monument for the ages as well, the astronomic clock known as Stonehenge, which brilliantly tracks the 19-year Metonic cycle (at which interval lunar months precisely fit into solar years) and all its smaller cyclic components. Each of these monuments is physically so substantial that its importance to the builders was clearly greater than that of an observatory, a mathematical formula or a clock. The observation of a *connection* between lunar and solar cycles and dramatic natural events and/or human social behavior would explain the dedication and commitment, indeed, the intellectual passion, of the builders. Why? Because such a connection would be so monumentally crucial both to understanding the patterns in the history of mankind and to anticipating future events.

There may be another reason that these structures are so unusually massive. After all, men don't undertake such projects today. We keep our present knowledge in perishable form, under the assumption that it will be around forever. Consider that a natural result of studying long term socially predictive phenomena is that one is eventually led to contemplate the great cycles of civilization and to realize that the present state of culture and society, whatever it may be, is ephemeral. Undoubtedly the architects of these monuments were intent upon preserving their most important knowledge for future cultures even if their own civilization were to collapse. These projects might have been designed, then, by scientists for a noble scientific purpose. For centuries, it was widely accepted that these structures were erected simply to satisfy the whims of a glory greedy monarch using slave labor and a mystical cult of robed animal sacrificers.* Such shallow and quickly adopted explanations demand an answer to the question, how many such anti-intellectual institutions have been known to ally themselves with scientists and build breathtaking triumphs of knowledge and engineering? Is the accepted conclusion really sensible? Or is it another example of the condescending attitude toward antiquity displayed by the aforementioned television astronomer? If a relationship between human social behavior and lunar cycles is ever formally established, perhaps a monument that clearly records and celebrates the link will be built some time during the next millennium.

If such a monument is built, much of the credit will go to Christopher Carolan, who appears to have re-discovered a substantial portion of a lost understanding of the correlation between the motions of the sun, Earth and moon and man's social behavior. Of course, correlation alone is not proof. The mechanism connecting phenomena must be identified as well. A physical explanation for any *immediate and direct effect* of lunar activity on mass human emotion has yet to be proved, although scientific studies have variously linked changes in lunar phase to changes in the Earth's magnetic field, the solar wind bombarding Earth and the electromagnetic state of living entities, suggesting that the idea of a link is within the realm of possibility. At minimum, it is a laudable feat that Mr. Carolan has established a correlation intricate enough to make a committed scientific inquiry into a mechanism worth undertaking. Having read Mr. Carolan's treatise, and having observed a number of his forecasts over the past three years, both errors and successes included, I am convinced that the Spiral Calendar could well prove to be a significant discovery in ultimately establishing a critical link between the cycles of time and human social behavior as evidenced in financial markets.

The Spiral Calendar and the Wave Principle are complementary tools in the field of market forecasting. On the one hand, the Wave Principle is unique in revealing valuable knowledge that can often be used to forecast *extent* (future price level, in market terms) with striking precision well in advance. On the other hand, the Spiral Calendar reveals valuable knowledge that can often be used to forecast *timing* with striking precision well in advance. *Both* bodies of knowledge possess a powerful utility *at the time* of a trend change. Both also pertain to *degree*, i.e., the size of expected trend changes, which is a critical aspect of the information, sometimes to the point of being of life-and-death importance to individuals and institutions, and upon occasion even to cultures.

In college, it's commonly understood that if you want to major in the easiest subject, you choose sociology. The reason is that modern sociology is not very scientific. In fact, it's so heavily laden with opinion and guesswork that only the truly lazy can't pass the subject with a creditable term paper. Currently published material on popular cultural trends is similarly vacuous and worthless, as such trends can be understood in their full significance only with an understanding of the Wave Principle, and now,

---

*That Stonehenge was built by Druids, certainly a more farfetched idea than presented here, was recently challenged by prehistorian Alban Wall, who demonstrated quite conclusively that it was the Celts.

perhaps, of the Spiral Calendar as well. I am quite certain that the 20th century will ultimately be known, as the 17th century is today with respect to the physical sciences, as the century that brought cohesion and grand vision to the field of sociology.

The two concepts together, plus whatever undoubtedly substantial knowledge remains missing, may ultimately, if civilization does not regress too far at any time over the next several centuries, produce a fascinating science of social man's intimate relationship with his universe. At minimum, as this book reveals, there appears to be evidence that human beings in social settings sometimes find the music of the spheres irresistible, and they are compelled, upon recognizing that everyone else is ready to do the same thing, to leap up out of their chairs and dance.

Robert R. Prechter, Jr., CMT
Gainesville, Georgia
June 28, 1992

PART I

FOUNDATION

CHAPTER 1

A DETECTIVE STORY

THE QUESTION

In what way did the 1987 stock market crash most closely resemble the 1929 crash? With the answer to this question I have formulated a method for forecasting periods of extreme emotional human behavior. These periods often occur at a time when markets, such as those for stocks or commodities, will change direction. This method is also applicable to mass human behavior in other areas such as political movements and trends. There are additional implications of my research, namely, the cause and structure of the larger forces that create the patterns of life and growth in the affairs of men.

Before I examine the question that led to all of these ideas, I will explain why I asked that question at all. In 1987, I was a stock option trader on the Pacific Exchange in San Francisco. There I stood in a "pit," a conglomeration of humans who often behaved more like beasts, hungry for a dollar, competitive, greedy. People yelled and screamed for any advantage available. Survival of the fittest was the accepted rule. In this environment many decisions are instinctive, intuitive or emotional. The conventional wisdom explains the movements of the markets as logical reactions or progressions of the latest economic insight or data bit, but the view from the pit is different. The "crowd" divides into buyers and sellers and the pit is where they meet. Their energy is like electric potential with two polarities. The trades are the sparks that jump the gap. Traders react by "feel." Sometimes this is an advantage, and yet when emotions prevail, it is a handicap. With time spent in a pit comes the ability to sense the pulse of the crowd. The most dramatic event for a trader to witness is the sudden and complete conversion of the crowd from buyers into sellers or vice versa, an event that occurs at important market turns. I frequently witnessed prices moving quickly in one direction while the commentary of the crowd cheered on. Prices accelerate and the commentary becomes even more definitive. "They'll never go down!" traders shout. Then, prices reverse and move just as determinedly in the other direction. The mood of the crowd has changed. They are convinced they have seen an important juncture in the market. Their change of heart is not a reaction to the change in the market, but rather a simultaneous occurrence. These are traders who, individually, will tell you they are behaving with logic and reason, yet will have a consensus opinion and then all change that opinion together, as if on cue. It is like watching a flock of birds flying in tight formation simultaneously reverse direction together. This is not how all markets behave at all times, but it is most evident in times of extreme emotion.

I was a six year veteran on the trading floor in late 1987 when the crash occurred. My own interest in observing the emotions of traders was sharpened by the single most extraordinary event in the lives of most current market participants. Here was emotion so great it was called a "panic," the first seen by my generation. It happened not just in one pit, but in many pits; not just on one exchange, but on many exchanges; not just in the U.S., but worldwide. Fear, panic and despair gripped millions simultaneously. Why?

This was not a unique event. It had happened before, most recently in 1929. Before the crash in 1987, some had seen parallels to 1929 and had profited handsomely. After the crash, newspapers were full of charts comparing 1987 and 1929. Figure 1-1 compares the Dow Jones Industrial Average for these two years. This chart shows all of 1929, January through December, compared to the same period in 1987. The comparison is amazing. Many analysts were captivated by the relationship between those two years, until the markets stopped following the same path. The subsequent years, 1988 and 1930, were not similar. Yet the fact remains that the pattern traced by prices in 1987 followed step for step what had occurred fifty-eight years earlier. When you look at these two charts, consider that they reflect a pattern created by the behavior of a group of individuals, and that each individual has the free will to buy or sell on any given day, and that these groups of individuals are separated by more than a generation. Yet, the patterns are similar. Why? How?

THE SIMILARITIES

There are four marked similarities in the charts of the two years. These four points give the comparison of the two charts their striking resemblance.

1. Both markets had a small correction that ended in late spring; May 31 in 1929 and May 20 in 1987.
2. Sharp rallies in both markets peaked in late summer; September 3 in 1929 and August 25, in 1987.
3. Both markets attempted rallies in the early fall, which failed to exceed the summer peaks. In 1929, the lower peak was on October 11. In 1987, it was October 2.

Figure 1-1   Pattern or Coincidence?

4. The crashes occurred in October. The 1929 crash was October 29. The
    1987 crash was October 19.

Each of these four points on the 1987 chart falls nine to eleven days earlier than
the same point on the 1929 chart. While these analyses point out the similarities of the
two charts, it is also evident that they are not strictly the same.

Now it is time for some detective work. What are the strengths and weaknesses of
this analysis so far? Figure 1-1 is a chart of the two years we are comparing. The chart is
interesting, but how is it made? There are *three* pieces of data that are critical to the
appearance of Figure 1-1. Two of the pieces are obvious, the stock price data for 1929

and 1987. The third is not readily apparent, but is crucial to the appearance of Figure 1-1. It is the *calendar* that determines how the two data sets align. The chart shows the first day of trading in 1929 aligned above the first day of trading in 1987, etc. By aligning both charts at the beginning of the year, we are using the calendar as the yardstick of comparison. The fact that the similarities in the charts occurred at the same time of year is what makes it most interesting. If one crash had occurred in March and the other in October, the shape of the charts may still be similar, but the comparison would no longer be as striking. *The similarity in the two charts is greatly a function of the calendar.* The examination of the exact dates of the similarities also uses the yardstick of the calendar as the absolute against which conclusions are drawn. The questions I wanted answered were, "Is *this* calendar the proper yardstick?" and "What would happen if the two years of trading data are compared with some other method of counting time?"

ON CALENDARS

The calendar we use is the Gregorian calendar. It is an improved version of the Julian calendar named for Julius Caesar. Our calendar, with its Roman origin, does a very good job of keeping time. The time it keeps is solar time, the rotation of the earth around the sun once every 365.25 days. There are other units of time a calendar could use. Ancient calendars usually measured the time it takes for the moon to circle the earth relative to the sun. Most calendars measure one type of time accurately and then approximate the other type of time. Our solar calendar approximates lunar time with its month, but this is an inaccurate measurement of lunar time. To distinguish between the modern month, which is 1/12th of a solar year, and the ancient month, which is one moon, I will use the term "moon" for the ancient month and "month" in its present context as a fraction of a solar year.

	1929		1987	
	Solar Calendar	Lunar Calendar	Solar Calendar	Lunar Calendar
Spring Low	31 May	2nd moon 22nd day	20 May	2nd moon 23rd day
Summer High	3 September	6th moon 1st day	25 August	6th moon 2nd day
Fall High	11 October	7th moon 9th day	2 October	7th moon 10th day
Crash	29 October	7th moon 27th day	19 October	7th moon 27th day

Table 1-1

Yom Kippur
9-25-93
New Moon was
3-16-91 + 927
DAYS
= 9/28/93

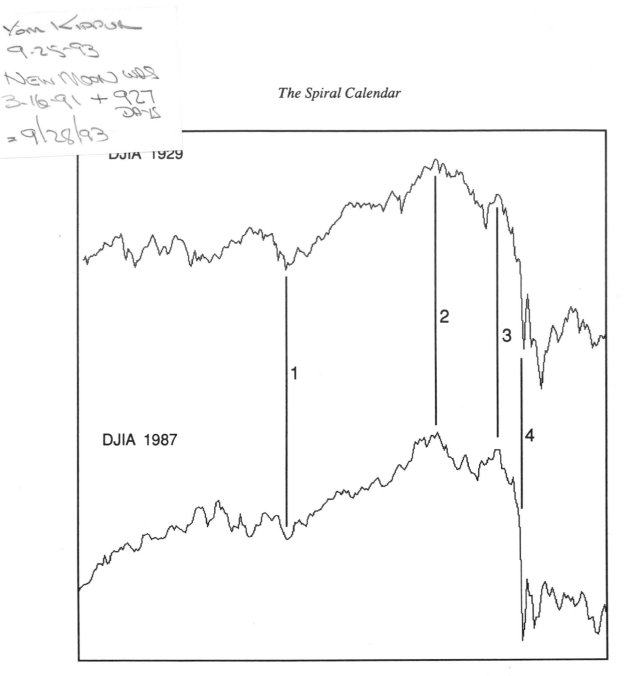

Figure 1-2 The two markets aligned with a lunar calendar.

The Jewish calendar is a lunar calendar, which is still in use to mark religious holy days. One of the holy days, Yom Kippur, fell exactly on the third point of the four market similarities in 1987, the fall market top. There is an old stock market adage, "buy on Rosh Hashanah (another holy day), sell on Yom Kippur." Selling stocks on Yom Kippur in 1987 was a very good thing to do. My desire to know when Yom Kippur fell in 1929 was the original impetus for my calendar investigations. The Jews borrowed their calendar from the Babylonians. A partial history of ancient calendars is explored in Chapter 8. In the Jewish calendar, the new moon is the first day of the moon cycle (month). The new moon near the spring equinox marks the first day of the first moon of the year. With this calendar I realigned the comparison of the 1929 and 1987 stock charts. The result is Figure 1-2. Shown also are the four points of similarity. Table 1-1

READ "BEFORE"?

16

shows the lunar and solar dates for the same four points. *The crash of 1987 occurred on the same lunar date as the crash of 1929!* The other three points each fall one day later on the lunar calendar than their 1929 counterparts. Within one day, the 1929 autumnal market top occurred on the Jewish holy day of Yom Kippur.

Could this be a coincidence? There are 354 days in a lunar year, 29.5306 days per moon times 12 moons. The 1987 crash could have occurred on any one of those 354 dates in the year, but it occurred on the same date as the 1929 crash. That's a 1 in 354 chance! Add to that the odds of the other three points falling on the same date plus or minus one day. They're very remote. It's more likely that you and I both win the lottery. I undertook this investigation on the belief, born in the experience of trading during the crash, that it was not a random event. The eerie parallels to 1929 spurred my curiosity. Now, here was a link between the two markets that was absolute and dramatic. In solar terms the 1929-1987 analogy was an intriguing coincidence. Now seen in lunar terms, the likeness is an empirical fact. Where there was similarity, there is now *sameness*. What appeared as a resemblance is revealed to be a *replication*.

Consider that the stock market chart of each year is a pattern or design created by hundreds of thousands or millions of people from their economic behavior through time. It has long been a wonder of nature to watch birds migrate or salmon return to spawn. They miraculously recreate their ancestors' patterns in minute detail without conscious knowledge of their actions. Here is evidence of the same activity in humans. In 1987, traders and investors danced to the same tune of speculation and panic that had played fifty-eight years earlier. Here also is the evidence of *what* was playing the tune that led those dancers. The phases of the moon provided the rhythms of greed and fear by which they bought and sold.

It was 1988 when I made the discovery of the lunar connection between the crashes. I understood immediately that this was an important advance in the understanding of both markets and man. However, it does not provide a method for forecasting market behavior by itself. It was a clue to the market's mechanism, and it pointed the direction I should look to for additional discoveries. It was some months before I made further progress. Most of those months were spent looking at that same pair of charts in Figure 1-2, one year positioned above the other, like a photograph of siblings; and I knew who the parent was on the other side of the camera: *Luna*.

It is not a new idea that the position of the moon and sun in the sky have influence on the behavior of man. In the West, it is traced to the Mesopotamians of 5000 years ago. To modern man, the idea is on the fringe of accepted knowledge, supposedly lacking "proof." I submit the extraordinary relationship in lunar time between the stock markets of 1929 to 1987 as the first brick in a wall of proof I will construct. Notice also, that it is when seen through the calendar of those same Mesopotamians, the evidence is made plain. The Mesopotamians will receive their full due in Chapter 8.

WHY 1987?

The question I needed to answer was, "Why did the speculation and crash of 1987 happen then and not in some other year?" My knowledge of the lunar relationship gave me no clue to that answer. I slowly came to understand that the chart I was looking at was not pointing me towards the next piece of the puzzle. I was looking at 1929 and 1987 as isolated years. I needed to look at the entire time span of stock price movements. *It was the interval of time in between that was the key.* Before, I focused on each of the four points being at the exact same lunar calendar point. Now, I saw the similarity in a different way.

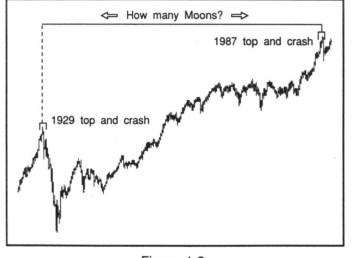

Figure 1-3

The distance in time from the spring low of 1929 to the spring low of 1987 was the same as the distance in time from the 1929 top to the 1987 top. This was also the same as the distance from the 1929 fall peak to the 1987 fall peak, and again the same as the distance from crash to crash. The two years had to be seen in a different way to be understood. This time span also needed a fresh perspective. It wasn't important that fifty-eight years separated these charts. It wasn't important how many days separated these charts. Weeks and months also weren't relevant. The question was, *how many moons separated these events?* See Figure 1-3 and Table 1-2.

Each event in 1987 occurred approximately 717 moons from the analogous point in 1929. The average of the four distances is 717.03. I felt that if there were a larger pattern to be found, this number should turn out to be significant. My first inclination was to check if it was a Fibonacci number. I first learned of Fibonacci numbers in high school. I next encountered them and the related golden section in my collegiate studies of ancient art and architecture. My third experience with Fibonacci numbers came through the work of R.N. Elliott and Robert Prechter and their analysis of the stock market. Yet 717 is not a Fibonacci number. I wondered if 717 might be some permutation of a Fibonacci number, maybe a multiple or a square root. With calculator and pencil in hand, I proceeded through the sequence of Fibonacci numbers. When I entered the 29th Fibonacci number, 514,229, into the calculator and pressed the square root button -- there

Distances from market turns 1929 to market turns 1987, in moons.						
Spring Low;	From	2nd moon 22nd day	to	2nd moon 23rd day	=	716.99 moons
Summer High;	From	6th moon 1st day	to	6th moon 2nd day	=	717.05 moons
Fall High;	From	7th moon 9th day	to	7th moon 10th day	=	717.05 moons
Crash;	From	7th moon 27th day	to	7th moon 27th day	=	717.02 moons

Table 1-2

was 717.0976. My first thought then is still very clear in my memory: "The world is a very beautiful place."

This was the second discovery my detective work had produced. These discoveries are empirical facts linking the two great financial panics of this century with concrete external phenomena, moon phases and Fibonacci numbers.

The next two chapters will take us away from the main topic, forecasting emotional market behavior, in order to obtain a foundation of knowledge about the moon and Fibonacci numbers. This is necessary for the ideas that will follow.

Chapter 2

Luna

Moon, Sun and Earth.

What are the phases of the moon? Why does the moon sometimes appear larger in the sky? Why are eclipses occasional and not once a month, excuse me, once a moon? What follows is an overview of the movements of the moon, sun and earth and the time periods they represent.

The unit of time of primary interest to us is the one marked by the phases of the moon, called a lunation. It is the time elapsed from full moon to full moon or new moon to new moon.

The moon is full when it is on the opposite side of the earth from the sun. The side of the moon that faces the sun is therefore the same side that is facing the earth, giving us a fully illuminated view of the moon. As the moon orbits the earth, it travels around to be on the same side of the earth as the sun. At this time, the side of the moon that is facing the earth is facing away from the sun. This side is in shadow, and we cannot see it. The effect is called the "new moon." See Figure 2-1. The term new moon comes from the ancients, who would watch the moon shrink to a sliver before disappearing or "dying." After three days, the reemerging moon was called new. The new moon is aligned too closely with the sun to view, not only on the day of the new moon, but usually the day before and the day after as well, hence three days.

The period of time from new moon to new moon is 29 days, 12 hours, 44 minutes and 2.8 seconds or 29.5306 days. This is the *synodic* month, which I will refer to simply

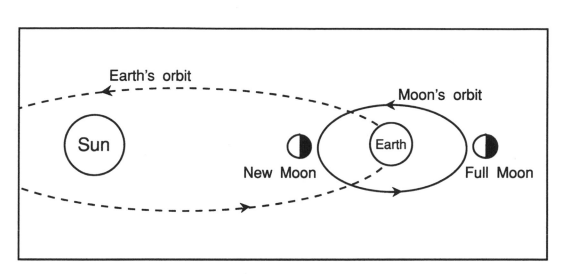

Figure 2-1

as a "moon." It is not the time it takes for the moon to orbit the earth. That is 27.3216 days, called the *sidereal* month. To understand the difference, start at a full moon. Here, the moon is opposite the sun, with the earth in between. In 27 days the moon will have completed one revolution around the earth, but the earth will also have journeyed farther in its course around the sun. The moon needs to orbit an additional two days, the difference between the synodic and sidereal month, to realign with the earth and sun for the next full moon.

The point to emphasize is that we usually consider the phases of the moon to be the product of the motion of the moon. Primarily they are, but there are three contributors to the phases, the sun, earth and moon. The movements of *the three combine to produce one* unit of time, a lunation.

Eclipses occur when the sun, earth and moon align so that the earth casts its shadow on the moon or vice versa. In a lunar eclipse, the earth casts its shadow on the moon. This can only occur at the full moon. A solar eclipse is the moon passing between the earth and sun at the new moon and casting its shadow on the earth. Eclipses do not happen at every new and full moon because the moon orbits the earth at an angle.

The plane on which the earth orbits the sun is the elliptic. The moon orbits the earth on a plane that tilts from the elliptic at an angle of 5° 8'. The moon crosses the elliptic twice in its orbit. The points of crossing are the nodes. The moon must be near a node and at new or full moon for an eclipse to occur. In Figure 2-2, the new moon is below its node, so there is no eclipse. The time it takes for the moon to travel from a node then back to the same node averages 27.2122 days. That is the *nodical* or *draconic* month.

The path the moon takes around the earth is an irregular ellipse. The earth is not in the center of the ellipse, making the moon move periodically closer to, then farther from, the earth. The point of the moon's closest approach to earth is the perigee, and the

21

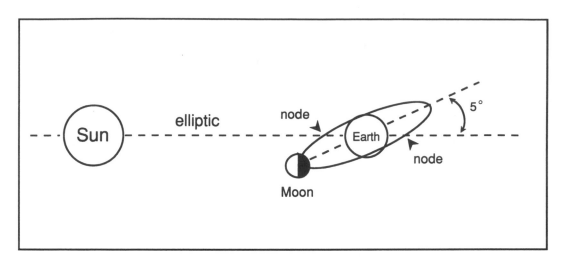

Figure 2-2

farthest is the apogee. The time it takes the moon to go from perigee to perigee or apogee to apogee averages 27.5545 days, the *anomalistic* month. At perigee, the moon appears 14% larger in the sky than at apogee.

All of these time periods, synodic, nodical, sidereal and anomalistic are averages. Any single time unit will vary from the average. The orbit of the moon is subject to gravitational pulls from other planets, as well as changes in velocity that effect these time units. The primary time unit of our concern is the synodic month. Over the centuries it has gradually lengthened as the moon very slowly moves away from the earth.

The other moon cycle that will concern us somewhat besides the synodic is the saros cycle. This is the 6585.32 day or 18 year, 11 day eclipse cycle. A saros marks the time when the moon has traveled a whole number of synodic, nodical and anomalistic months and solar years. After 6585 days, the moon, earth and sun will return to nearly the exact positions relative to each other, usually causing another eclipse. (SOLAR ECLIPSE)

Another interesting time unit is the lunar day. This is the time it takes the moon to appear at the same point above the earth, 24 hours and 50 minutes. The difference between this and the 24 hour rotation of the earth is similar to the difference of the synodic and sidereal months. If the moon is above a certain point on the earth, after 24 hours the earth will rotate back to that same point. The moon, however, will have moved further on its own orbit, which means the earth must revolve an additional 50 minutes to position the moon above that same point on the earth. The lunar day is the source of the main time period of the tides. High and low tides occur twice every lunar day, once every 12 hours and 25 minutes.

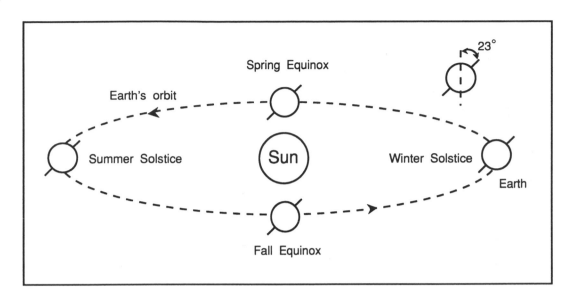

Figure 2-3

Sun and Earth

The earth completes one revolution around the sun every 365.249 days, the solar year. The polar axis, on which the earth spins, tilts from the perpendicular of the earth-sun elliptic at an angle of 23° 26'. Figure 2-3 shows the tilt in the axis changes relative to the sun throughout the earth's orbit. At the winter solstice, the first day of winter (around December 22), the North Pole is at its farthest point from the sun. The summer solstice (around June 21 in the Northern hemisphere) is when the North Pole is at its nearest inclination to the sun. The equinoxes mark the first day of spring and fall (about March 21 and September 22). At these points, neither axis is closer to the sun. The lengths of day and night are equal. Note that the tilt of the earth does not change with the seasons, just the orientation of the tilt toward or away from the sun.

Like the moon's orbit, the earth's orbit of the sun is an ellipse with the sun not at the center. The earth is at times closer to the sun. The point of closest approach is the *perihelion*, which occurs in January. The *aphelion,* the point when the earth is farthest from the sun, occurs in June.

JULY

Gravity

If I am to consider which forces related to the movements of the moon, sun and earth could possibly effect the emotional behavior of market participants, gravity is a likely starting point. I am not going to detail the physics, just relate how the previously described movements fit the gravitational picture.

Gravitational attraction varies inversely with the square of the distance between two objects. The strongest attraction we feel, other than the earth's, is from the moon. The sun is the next strongest pull, then the planets. This attraction is evident in the tides. The factors affecting the pull of the tides are proximity and alignment. The alignment at new and full moons causes higher tides. The sun, moon and earth align on a plane when the moon is at a node. The result is higher tides. Higher tides also occur when the moon is closer at perigee and when the sun is closer to the earth at perihelion. The highest tides occur when all these bodies are at maximum proximity and alignment.

MOON AND MAN

The connection between human life and the moon has been recognized for thousands of years. According to mythologist Joseph Campbell, the oldest evidence for an understanding by men and women of the significance of the moon is a stone age figurine from the South of France, which is about 17,000 years old.[1] In the figure, a woman holds a crescent shaped horn in her right hand. The other hand rests on her belly. The crescent shape has thirteen marks on it. It is suggested that the horn refers to the moon. The hand on the crescent and the hand on the belly show an understanding of the link between the moon and the fertility cycle. The thirteen markings represent the number of lunations in a year and the number of days from the first appearance of the new moon to the full moon. The moon has been looked to since as a device for counting and as the source of the reproductive cycle.

We can trace how these ideas have come down to us with linguistics, the study of language. Our word, month, derives from the Anglo-Saxon *mona*, meaning moon. The words menses, menstruation and menopause all have their root in *meno*, Greek for month. The menstruation cycle in women approximates the lunar cycle. Do not underestimate how important this is. The reproductive cycle is the starting point of human life. If there were no reproductive cycle, there would be no human life. Our language reflects this understanding. The base unit of time that defines the human life cycle is the moon.

The stone age figurine also makes reference to the moon as a device for counting. Our word measure is derived from *mas*, an ancient word for moon. The moon was the ancient measure of time.

Lunatic and lunacy are words that indicate a link between human behavior and the moon. They derive from the Latin word for moon, *luna*. We think of lunacy as a synonym for insanity. The words originally had different meanings. Someone who was insane was always crazy, while a lunatic was crazy only during certain lunar phases, usually the full moon or new moon.

---

[1]*Mystery of the Full Moon*-Public Media Video-1986.

This chapter is not the place to examine the accumulated evidence that lunar activity affects human behavior. However, a few examples deserve mention. I direct the reader to the bibliography for further information, particularly Katzeff's *Moon Madness*.

Arnold Leiber studied the timing of murders and aggressive behavior in Dade County Florida.[2] He found that murders and aggressive behavior peaked at the full moon and again immediately after the new moon. His work was criticized by other scientists who could not replicate the results. Leiber pointed out that his critics had used the time of death, which could be days later, and not the time of injury as the basis for their conclusions. It was the time of injury that correlated with the lunar phases. Injuries, presumably, are more likely to be sustained when a person is thinking more emotionally than "normal."

Ice hockey is a violent sport known for its emotional aggression and fighting. Katzeff reports that a study of the 1976-1977 season of the World Hockey Association showed that penalty minutes served by players on the night of the full moon were 33% higher than the previous night.[3]

Sir Matthew Hale argued in the 1600s that lunacy was caused by change in the moon's phases, *particularly at the solstices and equinoxes*.[4] A link between the effect of a particular lunar phase and its proximity to a solstice or equinox will play a part in my later investigations of economic behavior.

Chronobiologists study the timing of biological rhythms. They have found that the natural time unit of the human clock is the lunar day of 24 hours 50 minutes.[5] When humans are deprived of seeing the light and dark cycle of the solar day, their sleep cycle lengthens to approximate the lunar day. This explains why jet lag is noticeably worse for travelers flying East than West. If you cross three time zones going East, your day will be twenty-one hours long, three hours and fifty minutes shorter than the natural lunar day. If you travel three hours West, your day will be twenty-seven hours long, two hours and ten minutes longer than the lunar day. The adjustment for your internal clock will be less on westerly travel by one hour and forty minutes.

THE MOON AND OTHER LIFE

Lunar rhythms are present in non-human life forms. Aquatic life, with its close connection to the tides, is one example. Feeding time for most shellfish is according to tidal cycles. The question is, are the shellfish responding directly to the lunar pull or to the tide, which is a response to the lunar force?

---

[2]*Leiber*. pp 23-25.
[3]*Katzeff*. p 184.
[4]*Ibid*. p 9.
[5]*Wall Street Journal*. 10 April 1990. p 1.

In the 1950s, Frank Brown, a professor at Northwestern University, set out to answer this question. He took a tray of oysters from New Haven, Connecticut and brought them to Evanston, Illinois. They were fitted with pressure sensitive devices to record the opening of the shell at feeding time. For ten days, they continued to feed at the time of the high tides in New Haven. Then they stopped. The oysters, in unison, began to feed at the times that would have been high tide in Illinois, if there had been an ocean there.[6] He concluded that the oyster must be taking its feeding cues directly from the tidal pull of the moon, and not from the flow of the tide.

Many marine creatures feed and/or spawn according to lunar rhythms. The palolo worm, which lives in the ocean near Fiji, spawns on a given lunar date, seven days after the full moon of October or November. This is an example of life being regulated by both the lunar and solar calendars. The moon must be in the right phase *and* the sun must be at the right time of year for the spawning to take place.

SUMMARY

1. The primary time unit, the synodic month, lunation or moon is 29.5306 days.
2. Ancient man believed in the connection between life and the moon. This observation survives in our language.
3. Modern science has documented the long perceived connections between reproduction and the moon, and behavior and the moon.

---

[6]Palmer, Brown, Edmunds. *Introduction to Biological Rhythms*. Academic Press. New York 1976 pp. 215-216.

CHAPTER 3

FIBONACCI & ϕ

THE OTHER LEONARDO

Renaissance means rebirth. In Italy, the "rebirth" was the rediscovery of the knowledge of the ancients that was lost in the Dark Ages. In the fields of art and science, we think of Leonardo da Vinci as the supreme figure of the Renaissance. His age, the Quartrocento, or fifteenth century, epitomizes the Renaissance image. In mathematics, the Renaissance had occurred two-hundred fifty years earlier, and the central figure was the other Leonardo, Leonardo da Pisa, known also as Filius Bonacci, meaning "son of Bonaccio," shortened to Fibonacci.

In the arts, the Renaissance was propelled by the excavation of Greek and Roman artifacts, which gave contemporary artists their inspiration. There was no great mathematical tradition of the Romans to rediscover. The mathematics of the Greeks, primarily the geometry of Pythagoras, had originated with the Egyptians. Through the Dark Ages, mathematical knowledge was preserved and expanded by the Arabs and the Indians. Fibonacci received part of his education in Egypt, where his father conducted business. There he was exposed to the mathematical traditions of the Arab world, which he introduced to Europe.

Fibonacci's greatest contribution was the introduction of Arabic numerals and the place value system. In the decimal place value system, each numeral's value is determined by its place relative to the decimal point. The second digit to the left of the decimal point is worth ten times the same digit in the first position and one tenth the value of that digit in the third position, etc. The place value system greatly facilitates

n	F_n
1	1
2	1
3	2
4	3
5	5
6	8
7	13
8	21
9	34
10	55
11	89
12	144
13	233
14	377
15	610
16	987
17	1597
18	2584
19	4181
20	6765
21	10946
22	17711
23	28657
24	46368
25	75025
26	121393
27	196418
28	317811
29	514229
30	832040
31	1346269
32	2178309
33	3524578
34	5702887
35	9227465

Table 3-1

manipulation of numbers. If you have tried to multiply Roman numerals, you understand the advantage of the place value system. The introduction of this system to Europe produced the Renaissance in mathematics.

Fibonacci wrote three major mathematical works, the *Liber Abacci*, *Practica Geometrae* and the *Liber Quadtratorum*. One of these, *Liber Abacci*, contains the problem whose answer is the number sequence which bears Fibonacci's name. Here is the problem:

> Assume that a pair of rabbits start to breed at two months of age and they produce one pair, one male and one female, per month. Starting with one pair in the first month, how many rabbits will you have in one year assuming no rabbits die?

In the second month, you will still have one pair, as the rabbits are only one month old. In the third month, they produce one pair for a total of two pairs. The fourth month adds one pair to the total, making three pairs. In the fifth month, the second pair breeds also, adding two pairs, for a total of five pairs. After twelve months, there will be 144 pairs of rabbits. Table 3-1 shows the answer to the problem for the first thirty-five months. The left column, labeled *n*, is the number of months and the right column is the number of pairs of rabbits. Fibonacci himself did not investigate the properties of the sequence in any of his major works, though they have attracted the interest of mathematicians through the centuries. In the nineteenth century, mathematician Edouard Lucas named the sequence after Fibonacci.

PROPERTIES OF F_n

The Fibonacci sequence is denoted as F_n, where n is the sequence number and F_n is the corresponding Fibonacci number. In Table 3-1, where $n=12$, $F_n=144$, etc. The two most noteworthy properties of the Fibonacci sequence are: first, each Fibonacci number is the sum of the two numbers preceding it, thus it is an additive sequence; and second, the ratio of each Fibonacci number to its preceding number is alternately greater or smaller than the golden ratio. As the sequence continues, the ratio approaches the golden ratio,

1.6180339.., known also as ϕ (phi). This is true of all such additive sequences.

$$\frac{F_n}{F_{n-1}} = \phi, \text{ thus } \frac{F_{20}}{F_{19}} = \frac{6765}{4181} = 1.6180339...$$

An additive sequence is created by adding any two numbers together then adding the sum to the second number, etc. The Fibonacci sequence is the most perfect additive sequence, because its ratio will approach ϕ with fewer iterations. *144 + 233 + 233 = 610*

The golden ratio, ϕ, is the irrational number $\phi = \frac{\sqrt{5}+1}{2} = 1.6180339...$.

It can also be expressed as $\phi = 1 + \sqrt{1 + \sqrt{1 + \sqrt{1 + \sqrt{1 + ...}}}}$

This number and its inverse (.618...) are the foundation for the design of ancient art and architecture. The use of the Greek letter ϕ to denote 1.618 is a reference to the Greek sculptor Phidias, who believed in the number's role in determining proportion in art and nature. Phidias constructed the chryselephantine statues of Athena in the Parthenon and Zeus at Olympia. The latter was one of the seven wonders of the ancient world.

Here is a partial list of the intriguing properties of Fibonacci numbers.

- The sum of any ten consecutive Fibonacci numbers is divisible by 11.
- Every third Fibonacci number is divisible by 2, every fourth is divisible by 3, every fifth is divisible by 5, etc., the divisors being Fibonacci numbers in sequence.
- Consecutive Fibonacci numbers have no common divisor other than 1.
- 1 and 144 are the only Fibonacci numbers that are squares, and they are both the squares of their sequence number. The fact that there are no square Fibonacci numbers higher than 144 was proven in 1963 by John Cohn.
- 1 added to the sum of all Fibonacci numbers to F_n equals F_{n+2}.
- For every integer m, there is an infinite number of Fibonacci numbers evenly divisible by m and at least one exists in the first m^2 Fibonacci numbers.
- The square of any Fibonacci number will differ by 1 from the product of the Fibonacci numbers on either side. The difference alternates as plus one and minus one as the series progresses. Any additive sequence will have such a constant difference, but only the Fibonacci sequence has the number one as that difference.

This is expressed mathematically by $F_n^2 = (F_{n+1})(F_{n-1}) \pm 1$.

- For any four consecutive Fibonacci numbers A,B,C,D: $C^2 - B^2 = A \times D$.
- Every prime Fibonacci number except three has a prime sequence number.
- The final digits of the Fibonacci sequence repeat in cycles of 60. The final two digits repeat in cycles of 300. The final three digits repeat in cycles of 1,500, four digits in 15,000 and 150,000 for five digits, etc.
- There are two methods for calculating a given Fibonacci number without adding the sequence.

$$F_n = \frac{1}{\sqrt{5}}\left[\left(\frac{1+\sqrt{5}}{2}\right)^n - \left(\frac{1-\sqrt{5}}{2}\right)^n\right]$$

Rounded to the nearest integer, $\frac{\phi^n}{\sqrt{5}}$ will provide the exact Fibonacci number for n.

THE RATIOS OF ϕ

	Ratios of ϕ		Inverse Ratios of ϕ
ϕ	1.618	$\frac{1}{\phi}$	.618
ϕ^2	2.618	$\frac{1}{\phi^2}$	.382
ϕ^3	4.236	$\frac{1}{\phi^3}$	.236
ϕ^4	6.854	$\frac{1}{\phi^4}$	.146

Table 3-2

The ratios of ϕ and its inverse are the proportions of a Fibonacci number with its adjacent Fibonacci numbers. This is the rate at which the Fibonacci sequence grows. Alternate numbers in the Fibonacci sequence are related by ϕ^2 or $\frac{1}{\phi^2}$. The ratio of two Fibonacci numbers will approximate ϕ or its inverse raised to the power of the difference of their sequence numbers, n. Table 3-2 shows the first four ratios of ϕ. These ratios are themselves an additive sequence. Sir T.A. Cook in *The Curves of Life* calls this the golden series: .236, .382, .618, 1, 1.618, 2.618, 4.236... The ratios of this series are the same as the sequence itself, each number being 1.618 times the previous.

The following equations concerning the ratios hold true.

$$\phi + \frac{1}{\phi} = \sqrt{5} \qquad \frac{1}{\phi} + \frac{1}{\phi^2} = 1 \qquad \phi^2 - \phi = 1 \qquad \phi + \phi^2 = \phi \times \phi^2$$

The last equation is the most interesting, ϕ *added to* its square equals ϕ *multiplied by* its square. Phi's unique place among numbers as the bridge between addition and multiplication is why it and the Fibonacci sequence are ubiquitous in life and nature. Phi's source in the additive process of Fibonacci becomes the vehicle for the multiplying nature of life. The life process, reproduction, is another term for multiplication. In nature, like reproduces like, multiplying its forms throughout. Stock prices in 1987 were a pattern created by living things that replicated the pattern of 1929. Through the geometry of ϕ, we can understand how forms can be grown or reproduced.

THE GEOMETRY OF φ

The golden section can be described as the point on a line that will cut the line where the larger section will be in proportion to the smaller as the whole is to the larger, as shown in Figure 3-1. The proportion thus will be φ.

$$\frac{AB}{BC} = \frac{AC}{AB} = \phi = 1.618$$

The golden rectangle, Figure 3-2, is constructed by taking a square ABCD with sides equal to 2. From corner B, line BE bisects CD. By the Pythagorean theorem, BE equals √5. With a compass, create EF. EF + CE = √5+1. GF = 2. The ratio of CF/GF=φ. The smaller rectangle BGDF must also be a golden rectangle.

$$\frac{GF}{DF} = \frac{2}{\sqrt{5}-1} = \frac{2}{1.236...} = \phi$$

A smaller square DHIF can be drawn within this smaller golden rectangle, Figure 3-3. This will produce another rectangle, BGIH, which will also be golden. Each rectangle created is .618 the size of the next larger. The process also works in the other direction by *adding* successively larger squares to form golden rectangles, each 1.618 times the previous in size. The additive nature of this geometrical process is re-creating the same shape in logarithmically larger or smaller sizes. It can continue in either direction to infinity. The squares that are added to, or subtracted from, the golden rectangle are *gnomons*. A gnomon is a shape that, when added to a second shape, reproduces the second shape. This principle in nature is called gnomonic growth.

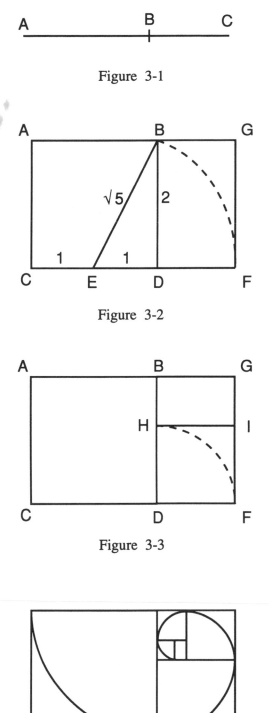

Figure 3-1

Figure 3-2

Figure 3-3

Figure 3-4

31

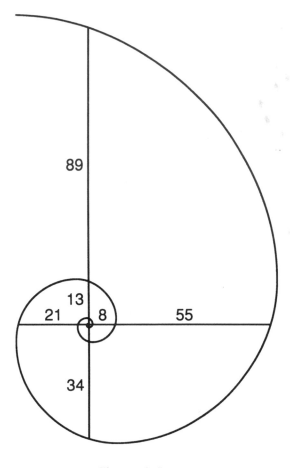

Figure 3-5

Drawing arcs within the squares of the nesting golden rectangles produces a golden spiral, Figure 3-4. The golden spiral is a logarithmic or equiangular spiral. The logarithmic spiral has a constant ratio or proportion between radii separated by the same angle. Figure 3-5 shows that the golden spiral has radii that are in ϕ proportion at right angles. The figure shows the radii in Fibonacci units. The golden spiral maintains its proportion as it spirals to infinity in each direction. There is no differentiation in shape between the smallest and largest parts of the whole. The spiral is a common manifestation of Fibonacci and ϕ in nature.

FIBONACCI AND ϕ IN NATURE

Spirals appear in seashells, pine cones, animal horns and patterns of plant growth (phylotaxis). The shell of the *Nautilus Pompilius*, shown in Figure 3-6, is nature's most perfect approximation of a logarithmic spiral. Among other shells, the *Haliotis Parvus* radii progress at right angles according to ϕ. The *Dolium Perdix* has $\sqrt{\phi}$ as the ratio governing its spiral progression. Spirals appear in non-living natural objects such as galaxies, and in nonliving natural processes such as hurricanes.

The growth pattern of the seeds of the sunflower form two spirals, one clockwise and one counter clockwise as shown in Figure 3-7. The number of spirals in each direction are adjacent Fibonacci numbers, usually 55 and 89 or 89 and 144. Very large sunflowers have been found that have 144 and 233 spirals. This is a striking example of the Fibonacci sequence in nature. The daisy forms a similar spiral pattern in the center of its flower. Fibonacci numbers in the petals for some flower types are shown in Table 3-3.

Vitruvius, the Roman architect and author of *De Architecture*, said, "Nature has designed the human body so that its members are duly proportioned to the frame as a whole." Studies show the proportions of ϕ are found in man. The average height for the navel of a man is .618 the total body height.[1] The human body, including the head, has a

---

[1]Fibonacci Quarterly. 17 4. *Golden Mean of the Human Body*. Davis, Altevogt. pp. 340-344.

Fibonacci five appendages attached to the torso. The hands and feet each have five fingers or toes. Our senses also number five, sight, smell, taste, touch and hearing.

No. of Petals	Flowers
3	Iris, Lily
5	Buttercup, Delphinium, Larkspur
8	Delphinium
13	Corn Marigold, Globe Flower, Ragwort
21	Aster, Chicory, Doronicum
34	Black-Eyed Daisy, Field Daisy
55	Black-Eyed Daisy, Field Daisy
89	Black-Eyed Daisy, Field Daisy

Table 3-3

The Fibonacci sequence has been found in the arrangement of the solar system. Planets with more than one moon have a Fibonacci correlation in the distances from the moons to the planet. A similar Fibonacci relationship holds true for the distance of the planets to the sun.[2]

φ IN THE ANCIENT WORLD

The φ proportion was known and revered by the ancient Greeks. Euclid solved the problem of finding the golden section of a line. Pythagoras incorporated the pentagram as the symbol of his Pythagorean society. The pentagram is constructed from the diagonals of a pentagon. Each diagonal cuts the others at the golden section. See Figure 3-8. Pythagoras was a philosopher as well as a mathematician. For the Greeks, the phi proportion represented the harmonious order throughout nature.

The knowledge of φ in ancient Greece extended beyond the mathematicians and philosophers to the artists and architects. The temples, the most sacred and enduring structures, were based on φ. The Parthenon's height and width form a golden rectangle. The temple of Poseidon at Paestum, one of the best preserved Greek temples, also has the golden section rectangle for its height and width. The length of the temple is exactly 2.618 times the width. The number of spaces between columns are Fibonacci numbers, five by thirteen. See Figure 3-9.

Pythagoras, like Leonardo da Pisa, traveled to Egypt. It is believed he learned his geometry from the Egyptians. The great pyramid in Egypt is built on the dimensions of the square root of phi. The ratio of the height of the pyramid to half its base is $\sqrt{\phi}$, as is the ratio of the apothem to the height. The apothem is the length from the top to the mid point of a side of the base. The ratio of the apothem to half the base is φ. These three proportional relationships are shown in Figure 3-10. The dimensions of the great pyramid are often described in terms of π.

---

[2]Fibonacci Quarterly. Oct. 1970. *Fibonacci Series in the Solar System*. Read. pp 428-438.

Figure 3-6

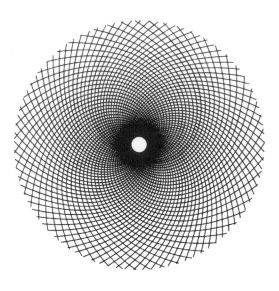

Figure 3-7

Figure 3-9

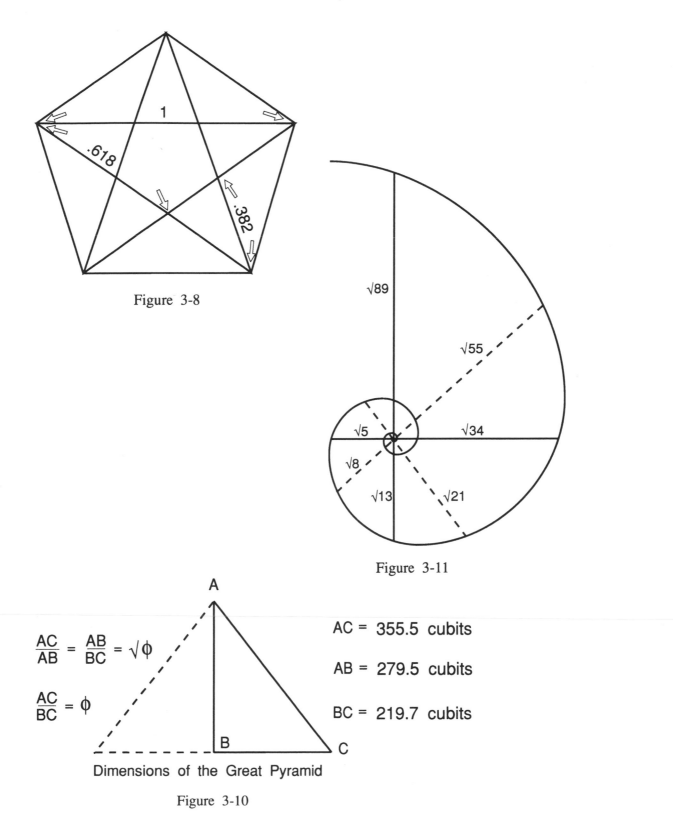

Figure 3-8

√89

√55

√5   √34

√8

√13   √21

Figure 3-11

$$\frac{AC}{AB} = \frac{AB}{BC} = \sqrt{\phi}$$

$$\frac{AC}{BC} = \phi$$

AC = 355.5 cubits

AB = 279.5 cubits

BC = 219.7 cubits

Dimensions of the Great Pyramid

Figure 3-10

This is possible because π is related to ϕ so that $\pi \cong \dfrac{4}{\sqrt{\phi}}$

Did the Egyptians use π or ϕ to design the pyramid? According to the measurements of Livio Stecchini, the pyramid was constructed using ϕ, with the π relationship a byproduct, and not the other way around.[3] The value of ϕ implied in the pyramid's dimensions is 1.61812. The implied value of π is 3.14418. The approximation to ϕ is closer to the mathematical ideal.

The Egyptian use of pyramids as monuments derives from the Mesopotamian ziggurats. The earliest versions of Egyptian pyramids resembled these stepped structures. Interestingly, the ziggurat at Ur in southern Mesopotamia was built as a temple to the moon. A study of ϕ proportions in art has found examples from Mesopotamia. The "Dying Lioness" relief from Ninevah ca. 650 BC, now in the British Museum, contains diagonals that cut the golden rectangle at the golden sections.[4]

The phi proportion was not just a mathematical entity to the ancients. They incorporated it into their philosophy, art and religions. They saw the connection between phi and the harmonic order of the universe.

$\sqrt{\phi}$ AND THE SPIRAL CALENDAR

The set of numbers that forms the basis of the theory of this book is the square root of the Fibonacci sequence, Table 3-4. The ratio that governs the proportion of this sequence is $\sqrt{\phi}$, 1.2720201... As the sequence progresses, the ratio of each number to its preceding number approaches 1.272... Table 3-4 depicts the square root sequence in two columns, labeled odd and even, to illustrate its *most important facet*. *The square root function applied to the Fibonacci sequence results in two separate additive sequences.* In each column of the Table, as the sequence progresses, the square root number becomes the sum of the two preceding numbers. The governing ratio of these separate sequences is thus ϕ. One sequence comprises the even sequence numbers, the other, the odd sequence numbers.

If we consider the square root sequence as a single sequence, Table 3-5 outlines the ratios that govern this set. Because alternate square roots of Fibonacci numbers are an additive sequence, the alternating ratios are the same as the set of ϕ ratios. The ratio of any two square roots of Fibonacci numbers is $\sqrt{\phi}$ raised to the power of the difference of

the sequence numbers, or its inverse. $\dfrac{\sqrt{F_{18}}}{\sqrt{F_{15}}} = 2.05...$ *or* $18 - 15 = 3$, $\sqrt{\phi^3} = 2.05...$

---

[3]Tompkins. *Secrets of the Great Pyramid.* pp 367-368.
[4]Fibonacci Quarterly. *The Golden Section and the Artist.* Hedian. 19 5. p. 407.

Figure 3-11 shows the square root relationships in the golden spiral. The radii separated by 45 degrees will have proportions of 1.272... In the figure, they are shown in units of square roots of Fibonacci numbers. Alternate radii are at 90 degrees and have φ proportions. The two sets of radii, diagonal (dotted lines) and horizontal-vertical (solid lines), are a visual representation of the two additive sequences of the square root of φ.

Our purpose in acquiring the knowledge of the proportions of φ, the

Ratios of $\sqrt{\phi}$		Inverse Ratios of $\sqrt{\phi}$	
$\sqrt{\phi}$	1.272	$\frac{1}{\sqrt{\phi}}$	.786
$\sqrt{\phi^2}$	1.618	$\frac{1}{\sqrt{\phi^2}}$	.618
$\sqrt{\phi^3}$	2.058	$\frac{1}{\sqrt{\phi^3}}$	.486
$\sqrt{\phi^4}$	2.618	$\frac{1}{\sqrt{\phi^4}}$	.382
$\sqrt{\phi^5}$	3.330	$\frac{1}{\sqrt{\phi^5}}$	.300
$\sqrt{\phi^6}$	4.236	$\frac{1}{\sqrt{\phi^6}}$	.236

Table 3-5

n	F_n	$\sqrt{F_n}$	
		Odd	Even
1	1	1.00	
2	1		1.00
3	2	1.41	
4	3		1.73
5	5	2.24	
6	8		2.83
7	13	3.61	
8	21		4.58
9	34	5.83	
10	55		7.42
11	89	9.43	
12	144		12.00
13	233	15.26	
14	377		19.42
15	610	24.70	
16	987		31.42
17	1597	39.96	
18	2584		50.83
19	4181	64.66	
20	6765		82.25

Table 3-4

geometry of the golden section and golden spiral, and the properties of the square root of the Fibonacci sequence is to apply these to the dimension of time. The original observation was that the connection between the market crashes of 1929 and 1987 is a unit of time based on the Fibonacci sequence.

The Spiral Calendar™ is a set of time units where the numbers of moons are measured in square roots of Fibonacci numbers. Table 3-6 shows the first 35 time units in the Spiral Calendar calculated for each of the three natural time units: moons, days and years.

The Spiral Calendar™

n	F_n	Moons	Days	Years
1	1	1.00	29.5	.1
2	1	1.00	29.5	.1
3	2	1.41	41.8	.1
4	3	1.73	51.1	.1
5	5	2.24	66.0	.2
6	8	2.83	83.5	.2
7	13	3.61	106.5	.3
8	21	4.58	135.3	.4
9	34	5.83	172.2	.5
10	55	7.42	219.0	.6
11	89	9.43	278.6	.8
12	144	12.00	354.4	1
13	233	15.26	450.8	1.2
14	377	19.42	573.4	1.6
15	610	24.70	729.4	2.0
16	987	31.42	927.7	2.5
17	1597	39.96	1180.1	3.2
18	2584	50.83	1501.1	4.1
19	4181	64.66	1909.5	5.2
20	6765	82.25	2428.9	6.6
21	10946	104.62	3089.6	8.5
22	17711	133.08	3930.0	10.8
23	28657	169.28	4999.1	13.7
24	46368	215.33	6358.9	17.4
25	75025	273.91	8088.6	22.1
26	121393	348.41	10288.9	28.2
27	196418	443.19	13087.7	35.8
28	317811	563.75	16647.8	45.6
29	514229	717.10	21176.3	58.0
30	832040	912.16	26936.7	73.7
31	1346269	1160.29	34264.0	93.8
32	2178309	1475.91	43584.5	119.3
33	3524578	1877.39	55440.3	151.8
34	5702887	2388.07	70521.2	193.1
35	9227465	3037.67	89704.3	245.6

Table 3-6

The first unit of the calendar is 1 moon, the time unit of the human reproductive cycle. The twelfth time unit is exactly 12 moons. At 354 days, it is eleven days short of a solar year, 365.25 days. These are the only Spiral Calendar units that are an even number of moons. The 15th unit is 1.1 days short of an exact two solar years. The 29th time unit, the one observed to connect 1929-1987, is 8.5 days short of 58 solar years.

In days, the 10th, 11th and 12th Spiral Calendar periods are 219 days, 278.6 days and 354.4. These numbers are close to the dimensions of the great pyramid in Egypt in royal cubits, the original measuring unit of the Egyptians. See Figure 3-10. Not only does the pyramid contain the proportions of $\sqrt{\phi}$, but the measurements closely approximate Spiral Calendar units in days.

The Spiral Calendar is a system of measuring time quite different from conventional clocks and calendars. Most numerical systems, having defined a base unit, proceed in arithmetic increments of that unit. *The Spiral Calendar moves in logarithmic increments.* The second number of the sequence is not twice the first and the third is not three times the first, as in an arithmetic progression. The human mind naturally prefers arithmetic methods of counting. The conventional analytic approach of time cycles (regularly repeating intervals) reflects this fact. However, it is the logarithmic function that has long been understood as the growth function, intimately connected with the life process. To apply this idea to the dimension of time reveals the patterns of life produced by the logarithmic building blocks of the Spiral Calendar.

PART II

MARKETS IN TIME

CHAPTER 4

SPIRAL CALENDAR REVEALED

The evidence of Spiral Calendar operation in markets is in the empirical measurements of past data. The quantity and quality of the evidence presents a dramatic case for the Spiral Calendar as the timing mechanism of market behavior.

717 MOONS: PANIC TO PANIC

It is a fact that the distance from market top 1929 to market top 1987 is the square root of a Fibonacci number of moons, as is the distance from 1929 crash to 1987 crash. Without further examples of these relationships, the link between Fibonacci, the moon and emotional market behavior would be a coincidence.

In 1799, a financial panic occurred on the European continent. Hamburg was the center of the panic, which Charles Kindleberger, author of *Manias, Panics and Crashes*, dates from August through November of that year. The 29th Spiral Calendar time unit of 717 moons is 58 years and 10 days. Fifty-eight years after the panic of 1799, the largest panic yet of the 19th century swept both sides of the Atlantic, beginning in August 1857 in the U.S. and reaching Hamburg in November. This is a second example of two panics separated by 58 years.

In 1942, the Dow Jones Industrial Average made a low on April 28 which ranks with 1932 and 1974 as one of the most significant bottoms of the 20th century. Though prices did not fall as low as in 1932, trading volume and the price of exchange memberships reached lower levels than in 1932. If we subtract 717 moons, or 21176 days, from April 28, 1942, the result is <u>May 5, 1884</u>. Daily prices of the Dow Jones

Averages are not available for 1884. However, Sobel, in his book, *Panic on Wall Street,* devotes an entire chapter to the events leading up to, and including, the first two weeks of May 1884. The panic of 1884 was called "Grant's panic." The former General and U.S. President lent his prestige to a brokerage house that contained his son's name, Grant and Ward. The Grant name attracted large amounts of public capital. The firm also borrowed heavily from the Marine National Bank for market speculations. When the market cracked, the bank failed and panic ensued. The market cracked on <u>May 3</u>, the bank failed on <u>May 6</u> and Sobel reported the panic as widespread on <u>May 10</u>.

PRECISION

Now we have three examples of panics or important lows separated by 717 moons: 1929-1987, 1799-1857 and 1884-1942. These examples have one characteristic that is most extraordinary. The measurement in each case is remarkably precise. Previous treatises on cycles in markets or business invariably refer to the average length of a particular cycle. Examples of the Kondratieff, or long wave, of approximately 55 years will include occurrences of 53 years and 57 years. with the proof of the waves' existence relying on an average. What I am demonstrating here is entirely different, a unit of time that covers *generations,* whose precision is accurate within *days.*

- • Precision separates the Spiral Calendar from all previous theories of time relationships in markets and is its most potent forecasting aspect.

GOLDEN SECTIONS

Are these examples portions of larger golden section, or spiral, formations? The 27th Spiral Calendar time unit, 443.19 moons, or 13,088 days, is .618 times the length of the 29th. Add this time length to the 1857 panic of August through November and you have June through September of 1893. The panic of 1893 is well documented; it too received a chapter's consideration from Sobel. We know from the Dow Jones averages, then in existence, that the low point of the panic of 1893 occurred on Thursday, July 27, within the June through September time window calculated from the panic of 1857. The total distance in time from the Hamburg panic of 1799 to the panic of 1893 is the 31st Spiral Calendar time unit. The panic of 1857 occurs exactly at the golden section of this distance.

1799-1893 = 58 yrs   *58/36 = 1.611*   *or √F 31 To √F 29*
1857-1893 = 36 yrs

If we add 13,088 days to the low of April 28, 1942, the result is February 26, 1978. March 1, 1978 was the date of the lowest Dow Jones Industrials price in the four years, 1976 to 1980. Here is a Spiral Calendar time unit 35.8 years long which measures from market low to market low, and that is precise to three calendar days. See Figure 4-1. This date can also be calculated by adding the 31st Spiral Calendar number to the panic of 1884. If we use May 10, 1884, when the panic was reportedly widespread, and add 34,264 days, the result is March 3, 1978, two days after the low.

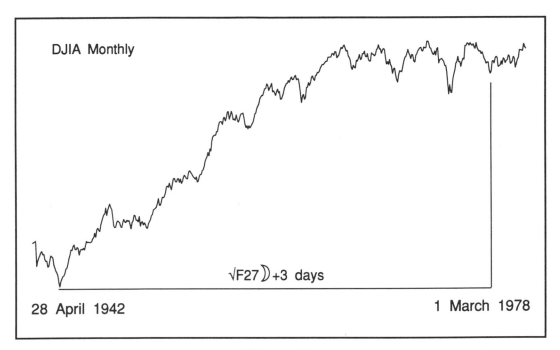

DJIA Monthly

√F27 ☽ +3 days

28 April 1942   1 March 1978

Figure 4-1

The 1987 top and crash, plus 13,088 days yields June and August of 2023. We don't yet know the outcome of this calculation. Instead of adding the .618 time unit to 1987, subtract the 1.618 time unit, the 31st, which is 1160.29 moons or 93.8 years or 24,364 days from the 1929 top. The result puts us in 1835, the year of a major market top. Stock prices did not return to their 1835 levels for over 25 years.

Farther back in time, the record of securities prices is less complete. The data for the pre-20th century charts in this book are from the Foundation for the Study of Cycles, which has reconstructed a monthly index of stock prices. This index accurately depicts the trend and major swings, but if a market is concentrated in one or two issues and those issues are not included in the reconstructed index, the data

Nomenclature

Spiral Calendar periods are denoted by the square root symbol followed by the letter F and then the appropriate Fibonacci sequence number. The moon symbol indicates that the unit of measurement is moons. The number following the moon symbol is the number of days the depicted distance varies, plus or minus, from the precise Spiral Calendar period.

√ F15 ☽ -2

The labeled distance is the 15th Spiral Calendar period minus two days. 729-2 equals 727 days.

43

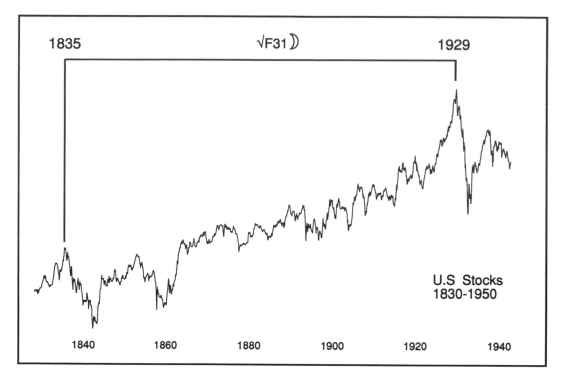

Figure 4-2

may not be reliable. I have combined this data with anecdotal and news accounts to form a more complete picture.

The 31st Spiral Calendar period subtracted from September 3, 1929, the day of the Dow Jones high, yields November 11, 1835. This date is not confirmed as a top by the reconstructed index, which peaked in June. The anecdotal evidence from Sobel differs[1]. He reports that the corner in the stock of the Harlem Railroad began in September 1835 and lasted "a matter of weeks," forcing the stock from 60 to 195. The scandal that accompanied the end of the squeeze "could not end the bull market of 1835." Stocks were "drifting lower in late 1835," he says, after the great fire of December consumed most of Wall Street. This account places the top no earlier than the beginning of October, and more likely later, within one moon of the calculated date of 11 November. It does not rule out that the top could have been precise within days. Figure 4-2 shows the great significance, or *magnitude,* of both the 1929 and 1835 tops.

The three examples each comprise three dates which, in turn, form three Spiral Calendar time units. The two smaller time units add together to form the larger unit, which is therefore partitioned at the golden section by the smaller units. See Figure 4-3. I call these contracting golden sections because the patterns appear to contract in length as they move forward in time.

---

[1]Sobel. pp. 58-59.

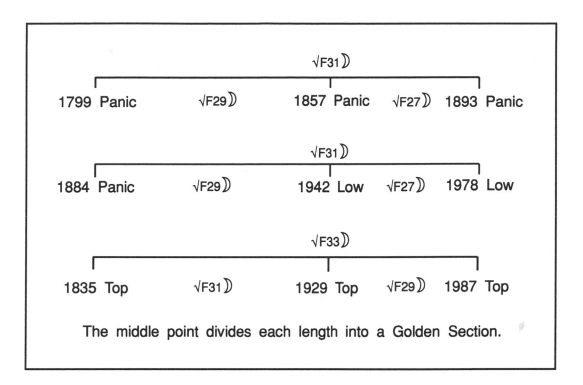

Figure 4-3

The implications of Figure 4-3 grow when you contemplate the golden sections relative to the size of their time span. In 1893, traders in New York were acting in a manner that forms a link with the behavior of traders in Hamburg nearly 94 years earlier. The participants of the top in 1987 were part of a much larger pattern that can be traced to 1835. A 152 year linkage is amazing. Do larger ones exist?

HOW BIG?

There is a Spiral Calendar relationship covering over two centuries with precision, which is awe inspiring. The Mississippi scheme and South Sea bubble of 1720 were among the greatest speculative manias and collapses of modern times. I will focus on the South Sea bubble in England. It inflated and burst in June-July of 1720. The Mississippi scheme was the French counterpart that topped in January.

White, in *Crashes and Panics,* relates that there are two historical accounts, Frecke's and Castaing's, of the time and price of the bubble's peak.[2] Frecke notes the highest trade in South Sea stock was at 1050 on June 24, 1720. Castaing records the

---

[2]White. pp. 42-44.

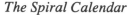

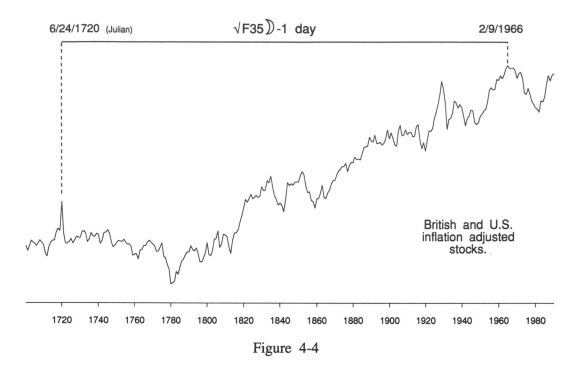

Figure 4-4

highest price as 950 on July 1. Castaing's price is less a 10% stock dividend, so both prices are roughly equal.

Before we can add Spiral Calendar time units to dates of this period we must adjust for changes in the calendar. The European continent had converted to the Gregorian calendar from the older Julian calendar in the 16th century. The English kings resisted the change, not wanting to give a Catholic pope credit for a good idea. England did not change to the Gregorian calendar until 1752, so the dates for the South Sea bubble top must be adjusted by eleven days, the difference between the two calendars. Eleven days added to Frecke's June 24 date is July 5, 1720. To this date, adding the 35th Spiral Calendar period gives February 10, 1966.

The U.S. stock market made an important high on February 9, 1966. The intra-day high of 1001.1 on the Dow Jones Industrial average was not exceeded until November 1972, over six and a half years later. By another measure, the stock high of February 9, 1966 has never been exceeded. Inflation masks the real value of stock prices. An accurate picture of the real value of stocks is obtained by adjusting stocks for the effects of inflation. This is done by dividing stock prices by an index of commodity prices or another inflation gauge. The market in 1966 reached its peak in a climate of low inflation. When stocks recovered to those levels in the mid-1970s, the prices were exaggerated by rapidly increasing inflation. Figure 4-4 shows nearly 300 years of stock prices adjusted for inflation. This "real," or "constant dollar," index marks the 1966 top as the all time high for stocks in modern times. The chart shows what we all know, today's investor buying the Dow near 3000 has less purchasing power and a lower standard of living than the 1966 investor buying the Dow at 1000.

If Frecke's date for the top is correct, the observed distance differs from the ideal mathematical Spiral Calendar number by 22.2 thousandths of one percent! The highest real stock prices of the 18th and 20th century are linked by a Spiral Calendar time unit that is **precise** to one day. Castaing and Frecke, taken together, corroborate a time frame for the 1720 bubble top that varies from the precise Spiral Calendar unit by no more than ten days in a period lasting over 245 years!

MAGNITUDE

A tendency emerges among the Spiral Calendar market relationships detailed thus far. The market tops of 1720 and 1966, separated by $\sqrt{F_{35}}$, were the real value highs of their respective centuries. The tops of 1835 and 1929, separated by $\sqrt{F_{31}}$, were not as important or as large in magnitude as 1720-1966. The lows of 1978 and 1942, separated by $\sqrt{F_{27}}$, on a chart do not appear to be as significant compared to the other examples where $\sqrt{F_n}$ was larger.

- There is a proportional relationship between the size of a Spiral Calendar sequence number, the *degree*, and the resulting *magnitude* of the market turn.

This observation enables a forecaster to apply a relative scale to market expectations; a very powerful tool, even more so when combined with precision.

SPIRALS IN TIME

I have demonstrated the existence of golden sections constructed of Spiral Calendar time units in the stock market. What other geometric patterns based on Fibonacci and ϕ exist? If there are logarithmic spirals, what do they look like in the single dimension of time? Figure 4-5 projects the two dimensional spiral shape into a one dimensional construction on a horizontal time axis. The center of the spiral becomes the point in time labeled *focus*. The time units, labeled in Fibonacci numbers, spiral out from this focal point. This spiral turns outward clockwise, producing what Cook calls a right-handed spiral. The pattern moves backward in time from the focus. A left-handed spiral will produce the opposite, time units spiraling forward, Figure 4-6.

The illustration in Figure 4-5 is a beautiful representation of the growth pattern of Fibonacci numbers. The pattern creates *three* sequences of Fibonacci numbers. The number 34 is part of the primary sequence in which every number in the sequence is anchored to the focus. The second sequence is the difference of adjacent numbers of the primary sequence, i.e. 34=89-55. The third sequence is produced by the difference of the alternate numbers of the primary sequence, 34=55-21. This is important because, if a given Spiral Calendar time unit lies on a larger spiral, there are three possible positions for it on a right-handed spiral. It may also lie on a left-handed spiral. This makes six possible locations for the focus.

47

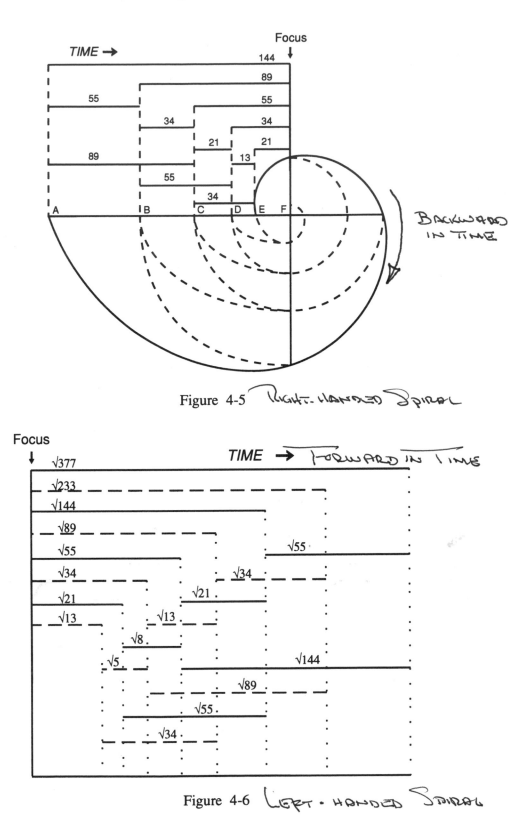

Figure 4-5 RIGHT-HANDED SPIRAL

Figure 4-6 LEFT-HANDED SPIRAL

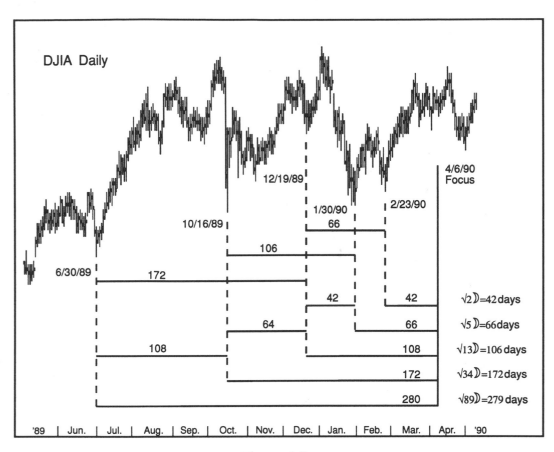

Figure 4-7

Figure 4-3 shows three golden section formations. In each, the time unit closer to the future is shorter than the other. That is, the golden section contracts as it moves in time. You can find three instances of particular golden section formations in Figure 4-5. For 55-34, there are ABC, BDF and BCF. The first two are contracting; the third, BCF, is expanding in time. On a left-handed spiral there are two expanding and one contracting examples of each golden section. Therefore, any given golden section has a total of three possible spirals and focal points. For a contracting golden section, two lie on right-handed spirals and one lies on a left-handed spiral.

The spiral of Figure 4-5 shows a single additive sequence. Figure 4-6 is a spiral in time constructed from the Spiral Calendar with both alternating additive spirals created by the square root of Fibonacci sequence. The units of the odd sequence numbers are shown with dashed lines, the even with solid lines. Like the single additive spiral, there are three separate sequences created in the structure. One is anchored to the focus, i.e. √34, the second is composed of alternate sequence numbers, √34=√233-√89, and the third by fourth alternate numbers, √34=√89-√13.

49

The reproductive nature of the Spiral Calendar creates replicas of shapes and sequences. With one piece of the puzzle, finding the larger spiral, if any exist, requires an understanding of the form it will take. These two charts are the road maps for the patterns we will encounter. How to find the spirals and foci will be covered later in Chapter 6. In the real world, some Spiral Calendar units exist as single phenomena, others group into golden sections, still others form larger constructions that do not have the regularity of the ideal spiral of Figure 4-5. Finally, there exist perfect spirals of incredible beauty and precision. I distinguish spirals from golden sections by the number of turns in the structure. Golden sections have three turns, while spirals have four or more. What was a golden section can become a spiral as more turns occur on the sequence. Other times, the pattern will stop after three turns, leaving only the golden section structure.

Figure 4-7 is a perfect spiral and, like a flawless gem, a rarity. Here the beauty of the logarithmic spiral meets the truth of a market created by millions of investors and traders matching wits and emotions, profit and loss, fear and greed, hope and despair. It is incredible that we can construct an ideal mathematical structure in Figure 4-5 and then find that exact structure in a striking visual pattern of stock prices.

The chart shows 13 months of trading in the Dow Jones Industrial average. The numbers on the spiral are the distance in calendar days from low to low and from low to focus. The legend at right reveals the odd sequence Spiral Calendar lengths in days. Note the *precision* with which the structure adheres to the ideal Spiral Calendar numbers. The focus, April 6, 1990, is not a market turning point, but it is the defining point for the five lows in the structure. Some points are connected to each other by Spiral Calendar units, but all points are connected by Spiral Calendar units to the focus. I use the date of the focus to name the spiral, making it the *April 6, 1990 spiral*.

The April 6, 1990 spiral is "perfect" because of its regular features.
- There are no missed turns. From the first turn in the spiral, every alternate Spiral Calendar number resulted in a turn.
- All turns are the same type. Here they are market bottoms.

The low of June 1989, the first in the sequence, is not as large in magnitude as the subsequent low of October 1989. The "mini crash" is of smaller degree on the spiral. The concept of magnitude would suggest it should have been less significant a market turn than the June low. However, the "mini-crash" is the larger magnitude low because it lies on two spirals. Spirals can nest together, sharing a common point between them. Figure 4-8 is a larger spiral, with one of the lows the October "mini crash." The degree, or sequence number, of the "mini crash" on the larger spiral, shown in Figures 4-8 and 4-9, is greater than any lows on the smaller spiral, shown in Figure 4-7. This explains why its magnitude is greater than the other lows on the smaller spiral. This larger spiral is also perfect. It consists only of lows, and every alternate Spiral Calendar point has produced a turn as of this writing. The turns of this spiral define the major pattern of lows of the

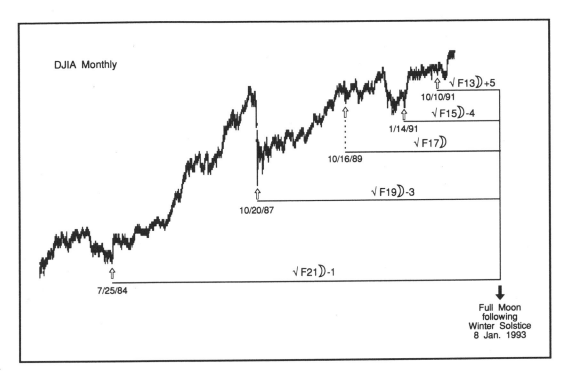

Figure 4-8

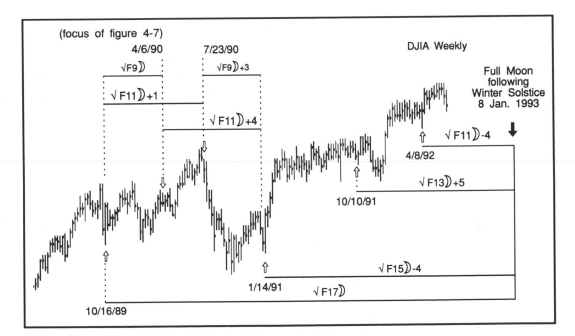

Figure 4-9

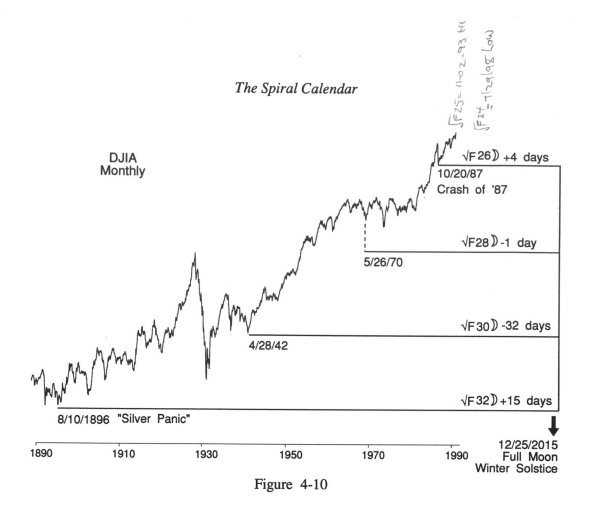

Figure 4-10

mid-1980s and early 1990s. The focus is January 8, 1993. Once again, the precision is amazing.

The smaller spiral shares more than the common "mini-crash" point with the larger spiral. The focus of the smaller spiral, April 6, 1990, cuts the distance from the mini-crash low and the January 1991 low at the golden section. See Figure 4-9. Those distances are themselves Spiral Calendar units. The smaller spiral nests in the larger spiral. The patterns are the same, the magnitude and degree are different. The larger spiral of Figure 4-8 shares a point with a still greater spiral, illustrated in Figure 4-10.

The great spiral in Figure 4-10 has its focus in the 21st century, December 25, 2015. Its first low occurred in the 19th century. It is perfect in that every alternate Spiral Calendar unit since the first occurrence has produced a turn and every turn has been the same, a low. The crash of 1987 is the point common to the two spirals. If the crash low had fallen precisely to the day on the January 1993 spiral, it would have been Saturday, October 17. The precise measurement for the December 2015 spiral is October 24. The print low on the Dow Jones in 1987 was October 20, effectively splitting the difference of the two spiral measurements.

There are some characteristics that set this greater spiral apart from the first two examples. These turns fall on the even sequence numbers of the Spiral Calendar, while the other spirals are on the odd sequence. Because of this fact, the focus of the January 1993 spiral does not lie on a golden section of the great spiral of December 2015. The

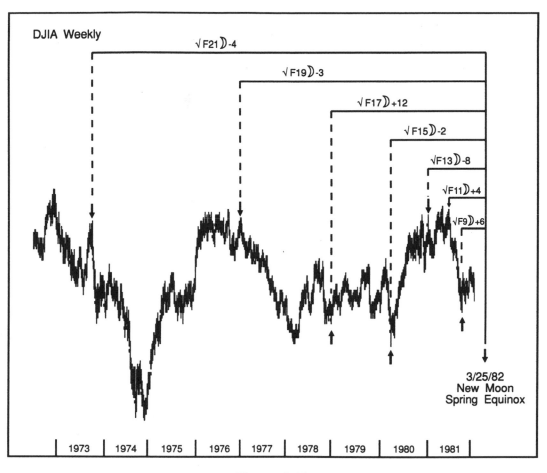

Figure 4-11

low of 1942 in this spiral is not precise. It varies from the ideal by 32 days (lunation + 3 days). Turns that lack precision I call *approximate*. I will demonstrate later how turns will cluster at points that are precise to one or more structures and approximate to others. Remember, the 1942 low falls precisely on a different structure, a golden section that includes the 1884 panic and the 1978 low.

THE FOCUS

- The focus of a spiral or partial spiral will tend to fall on a moon phase
  near a solar seasonal change, <u>and/or</u> an emotional market turning point,
  <u>or</u> a golden section division of a larger spiral.

Each of the spirals in Figures 4-8 and 4-10 has a focus that is the first full moon after the winter solstice. This combination of full moon and winter solstice seems to produce the most perfect of spirals that are associated exclusively with market lows. I have only found them to move backward in time, not forward. The second frequent focal

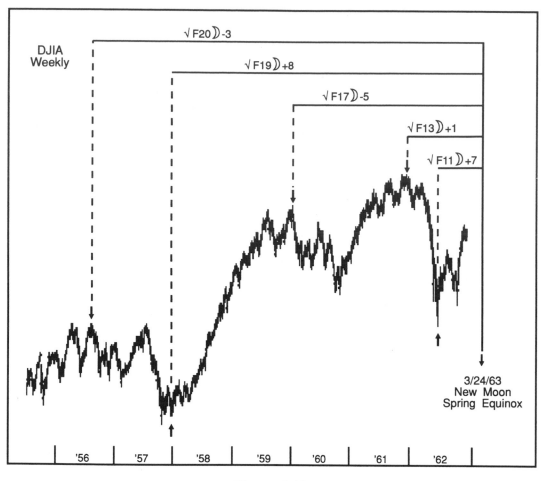

Figure 4-12

point is the new moon near (usually after) the spring equinox. This moon will produce spirals that move forward or backward. The forward spirals are of smaller degree, producing turns of smaller magnitude. These spirals produce tops or bottoms and can produce turns either on an alternating Spiral Calendar sequence (odd or even) or on consecutive sequence numbers. The new moon, spring equinox spirals will more frequently have missing turns, i.e. the pattern skips a beat.

Figures 4-11 through 4-14 show new moon, spring equinox spirals. The spiral with the focus of Spring 1982, shown in Figure 4-11, has turns spiraling backwards on the odd Spiral Calendar numbers. The spiral contains four highs and three lows, for a total of seven turns. Two of the turns vary from the ideal by twelve and eight days. These differences are too great to be precise. Figure 4-12 is a new moon, spring equinox spiral moving backwards from 1963. The turns reflect the odd sequence, skipping $\sqrt{F}_{15}$. One turn also falls on the even sequence $\sqrt{F}_{20}$. This spiral defines some of the major turns of the late 1950s and early 1960s. Figures 4-13 and 4-14 are forward spirals, using

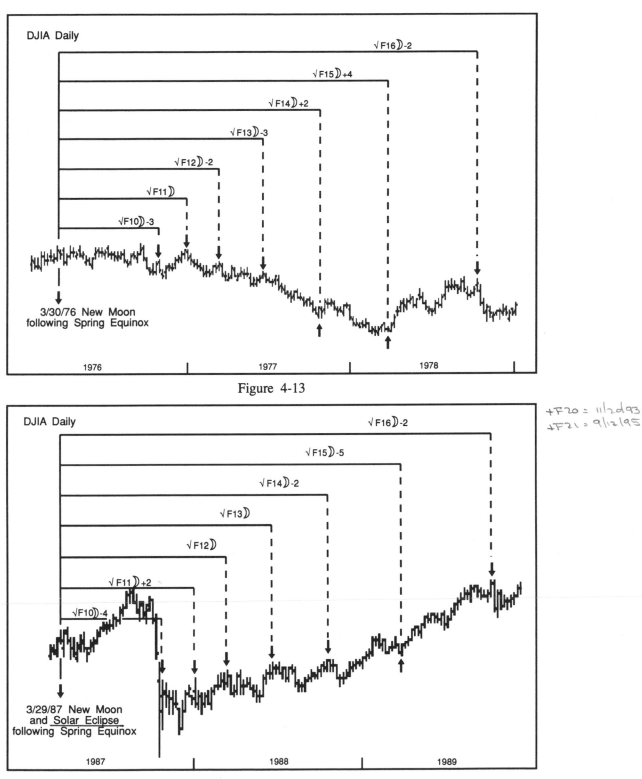

Figure 4-13

Figure 4-14

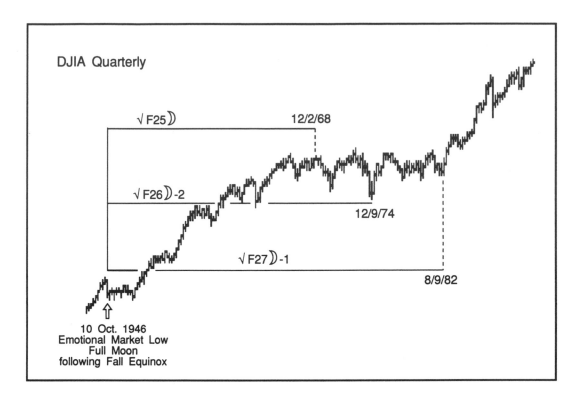

Figure 4-15

consecutive sequence numbers, from the new moon, spring equinoxes of 1976 and 1987. Both generated turns, mostly tops, on consecutive Spiral Calendar points. The spirals terminated at the October highs of 1978 and 1989, which preceded October mini-panics in both years. The focus of Figure 4-14 is an example of a focus falling on a lunar-solar alignment and near an emotional market turn. March 23, 1987 was the high for the advance decline line in the bull market from 1974.

An extraordinary forward spiral in magnitude and precision is shown in Figure 4-15. Here the focus is the full moon following the fall equinox. This is the only example I have found of this lunar-solar alignment producing a spiral. More important, the focus was a point of extreme emotional market behavior. The full moon of October 1946 was on the 10th. The market's closing low for 1946 was October 9. On the morning of the 10th, stocks traded lower still before recovering and closing higher. Figure 4-16 shows the daily prices for the summer and fall of 1946.

Emotional markets are one-sided markets. These are times when almost everyone is on the same side of the market. Panics are one-sided selling waves and manias are their buying counterpart. The advance/decline ratio is an excellent measure of one-sided extremes in markets. This is the ratio of the number of stocks that close higher on the day divided by the number of stocks lower on the day. Figure 4-16 contains advance/decline ratios for seven days in 1946. The six negative ratios on the chart are among the 100 most negative advance/ decline ratios from 1934 to the present. The two worst, 1:31 and 1:28, are ranked eighth and eleventh in a ranking of the 100 lowest ratios from 1934. This shows the extreme one-sided selling leading into the low of October 1946. On October 15, the ratio reached the opposite extreme of 28 advances to each decline, the second best ratio from 1934. The market low of October 1946 saw a dramatic change in the emotional sentiment of traders and investors. The

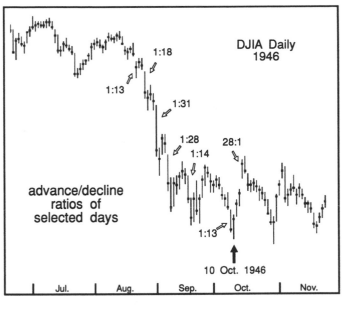

Figure 4-16

one-sided urge to sell was replaced with an equally one-sided urge to buy. The point of extreme emotional inflection was the full moon after the fall equinox. Look at the consequences of this point in time as the focus of a Spiral Calendar sequence into the future.

The spiral forward from 1946 produced the top of December 1968 and the lows of December 1974 and August 1982 on consecutive sequence points. The precision is uncanny. No point varies from the ideal by more than two days, even though 35 years separate the 1982 low from the focus. The three turns produced are arguably the most important turns of the 14 years from the late 1960s through the early 1980s. The magnitude of the turns is commensurate with the degree of the Spiral Calendar sequences. Here the beauty of the mathematical ideal joins with the truth of man's pattern of market behavior over decades of time.

The spiral forward from 1946 poses the logical question: why is the 1968 top the first point on the sequence? Why are there no precise relationships of smaller degree before 1968? In general, this is an issue of magnitude. Large magnitude events are connected with other large magnitude events by large degree Spiral Calendar relationships. The large emotional low of 1946 is not expected to relate to small turns close in time. I can offer no specific reason why $\sqrt{F}_{25}$ moons is the first sequence number and not $\sqrt{F}_{24}$ moons or $\sqrt{F}_{26}$ moons. Another example is Figure 4-4. The emotional 1720 mania was much greater than 1946. A contemporary described the trading scene in 1720, "As if all the lunatics had escaped out of the madhouse at once." This is consistent with magnitude in that the very large degree, $\sqrt{F}_{35}$ moons, is proportional to the size of the mania it measures from. The 1966 top is the first sequence to measure precisely from 1720. I expect that this turn will be part of a larger pattern, but there is no explanation for

57

why the 1966 top is the first relationship. The 1720 high, if Frecke's July 5 (Gregorian) top date is correct, occurred no more than one day from a new moon. This means, that as a focus into the future, 1720 was the new moon following the summer solstice <u>and</u> a very emotional turning point.

One of the golden section examples shown previously is part of a larger spiral. The golden section formation of lows, 1884 - 1942 - 1978, has three potential foci. The 1884 panic could be the focus of a forward spiral; the 1978 low could be the focus of a backward spiral; or, the spiral moves backward and the focus is 18-21 February, 2036. I will explain in Chapter 6 how this later date is figured, although it can be deduced from Figure 4-6. By calculating back from 2036, a spiral that has a split focus appears. The odd sequence dates measure back to 1978, 1942 and 1884. A second focus about 32 days later calculates using the even Spiral Calendar sequence to the high of November 1916, the panic low of June 1962 and the Kuwaiti war slide of August 1990. See Figure 4-17. Why the split foci? The even sequence focus best calculates as March 21-25. This is between the spring equinox, March 20, and the new moon, March 27. The focus of the odd sequence falls in the eclipse season between the total solar eclipse of February 11 and the lunar eclipse of February 26. The chart shows the precise measurements calculated from the dates shown.

The spiral exhibits good precision from each of the split foci. Moving forward in time, there is a marked dropping off in the magnitude of the resulting turns. The 1978 low is less significant than all of the previous turns. The August 1990 low did not hold for most averages, although it was the low for the year in bond prices and the utility average, the high price for gold and the point of maximum downside momentum in stocks. I expect this spiral's influence in the future will continue to lessen.

HARMONY

All Spiral Calendar units are not equal. Some periods seem to occur more frequently than others. This fact may be a function of how a certain Spiral Calendar unit relates to the natural units of time, moons, solar years and saros cycles.

- If a Spiral Calendar distance approximates a whole number of natural time units, it is in *harmony* with that time unit.

The 29th Spiral Calendar unit is almost exactly 717 moons (717.0976). This is *lunar harmony*. It is also almost exactly 58 years (57.9776). This is *solar harmony*. The 12th Spiral Calendar unit is exactly 12 moons, producing lunar harmony. The 15th Spiral Calendar unit is within one day of being exactly 2 years (1.99685 years), producing solar harmony. The effects of lunar and solar harmony are discussed in Chapter 5. The 27th Spiral Calendar unit is almost 2 saros cycles in length (1.98740). This is *saros harmony*.

Figure 4-18 demonstrates saros harmony at work. In May of 1901, a rising market fueled by takeover speculation in transportation stocks led to the panic of 1901 (shades of 1989!). *The New York Times* headline of May 10 read:

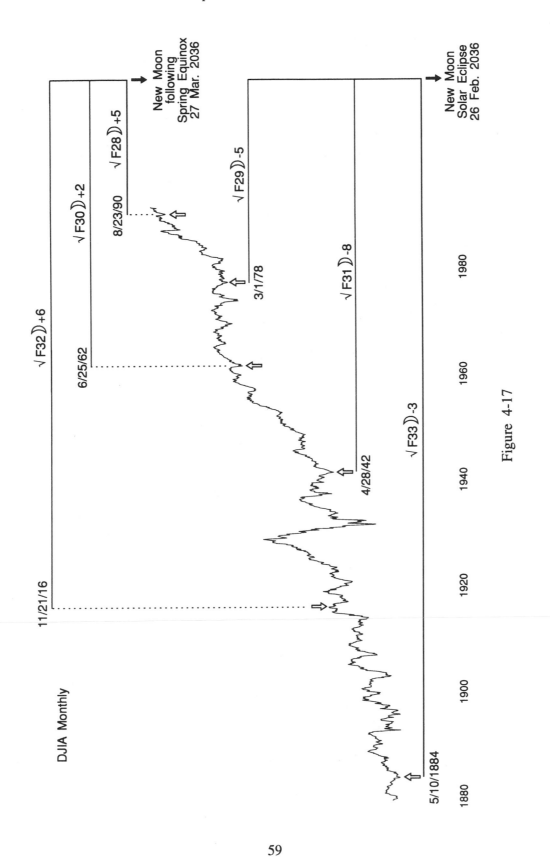

Figure 4-17

"DISASTER AND RUIN IN FALLING MARKET

Panic Without a Parallel in Wall Street

The greatest general panic that Wall Street has ever known..."

On that day, a short squeeze in Northern Pacific drove the stock from its previous day's close of 160 up to 1000 dollars per share. The stock then collapsed back to close the day at 325. The squeeze forced massive liquidation in other issues as speculators, who were short Northern Pacific, raised needed cash. This marked the end of the bull market of 1901.

The date of the panic, May 9, was after the lunar eclipse of May 3 and before the solar eclipse of May 18. This solar eclipse belongs to the saros series that produced the longest total solar eclipses of this century. Three had a duration of over seven minutes. The eclipses in this saros during this century were 1901, 1919, 1937, 1955, 1973 and 1991.

Figure 4-18 shows how the two market tops, 1937 and 1973, measure forward from the panic of 1901. The tops measure precisely using $\sqrt{F_{27}}$ moons. The tops do not measure from the eclipse of 1901, but from the date of the panic itself. The measurement is not that of two saros cycles, but rather that of the Spiral Calendar unit that is in harmony with the saros. We can see the effect of the eclipse cycle on the market here, but it is very important to understand that, ultimately, it is the Spiral Calendar that determines the pattern, not the saros.

The structure in Figure 4-18, in which the same sequence number repeats, is consistent with the spiral patterns we have seen. In Figure 4-7, you can see how each sequence number repeats. It is 108 days from the June '89 low to the October '89 low and then 106 days from the October '89 low to the January '90 low. If the saros chart is part of a larger spiral, its focus would be $\sqrt{F_{25}}$ moons subtracted from 1901 if it is forward, and $\sqrt{F_{25}}$ moons added to 1973 if it is backward. Placing the focus at those points yields no other significant relationships. The structure, then, is a partial spiral created from the occurrence of a panic in proximity to an eclipse and the Spiral Calendar number in harmony with the saros.

FORWARD VS. BACKWARD

It is arbitrary that I call spirals moving back in time, "right handed" and spirals moving forward, "left handed." Figure 4-5 could just as easily have a left hand spiral attached to the top of the time line to produce a backward spiral. I have found the backward spiral to be more common than the forward spiral. This is consistent with other forms in nature. Cook reports that in spiral shells, one type, which he calls right handed, is by far the more common. By applying this concept to time, we are raising a fascinating issue. The implication of the forward spiral, with its focus preceding the spiral, is of a past event growing into and affecting the future. This is not an easy concept for those who cannot believe that market events of 58 or 245 years ago could be directing the pattern of current trading. The implication of the backward spiral is even more controversial. In the backward spiral, the future focus seems to determine the course of

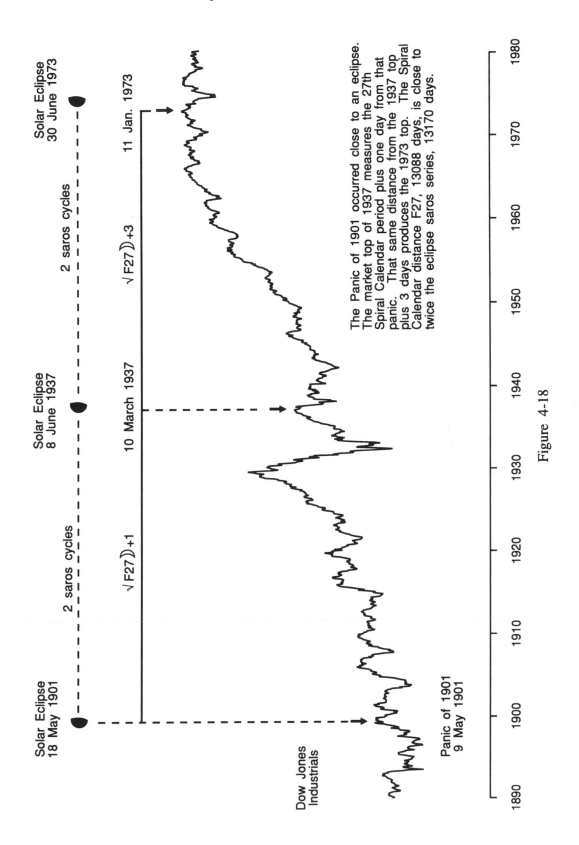

The Panic of 1901 occurred close to an eclipse. The market top of 1937 measures the 27th Spiral Calendar period plus one day from that panic. That same distance from the 1937 top plus 3 days produces the 1973 top. The Spiral Calendar distance F27, 13088 days, is close to twice the eclipse saros series, 13170 days.

Figure 4-18

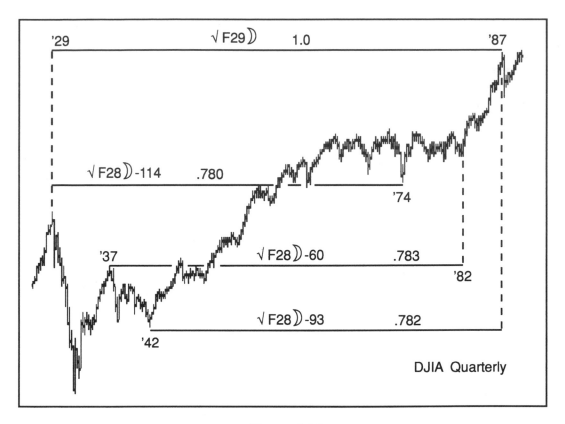

Figure 4-19

events in the present. It may be just an illusion that the future appears to affect the present. The additive nature of the spiral in the past is probably the ultimate source of the spiral's direction, not its focus. Nevertheless, it remains unexplained why the future focus tends to be a lunar phase near a solstice or equinox or a point on another spiral.

APPROXIMATION

There are Spiral Calendar relationships that are not precise, yet form striking repetitive patterns. Figure 4-19 shows three distances that approximate $\sqrt{F_{28}}$ moons. The variations from the ideal range from 60 to 114 days, or 2 to 4 moons. Each of the turns is precise to other sequences in this chapter. The chart also shows these lengths as ratios of the larger 1929 to 1987 distance. They are close to $1/\sqrt{\phi}$, .786.... Spiral Calendar relationships can seem confusing, as separate precise structures appear to bear no relationship to each other. The connection of these disparate elements *through approximation* further reveals the *structure and beauty* of the Spiral Calendar's patterns.

There is another explanation for why a turn may lack precision. A market turn can take more than one form. In addition to dramatic "spike" turns, markets may form gradual turns that take a "rolling" shape. The exact extreme of the gradual turn will likely occur on different dates in various indices. The turn may be precise in one index, but not another. Gradual turns are more likely to be market tops than bottoms.

SUMMARY

- Emotional market turns are connected by distances in which the number of moons equals the square root of Fibonacci numbers, forming the Spiral Calendar™.

- These lengths of times group together to form larger spirals and sections of spirals. A spiral is the shape created by projecting the square root of Fibonacci sequence onto the dimension of time. Figures 4-5, 4-6.

- Spiral Calendar relationships separating market events contain striking *precision* in their measurements.

- The *degree,* or sequence number, of the Spiral Calendar unit in a market time span is generally proportionate to the *magnitude* of the market event.

- The point at which a spiral anchors is the *focus*. The focus of a spiral or partial spiral will tend to fall on a moon phase near a Solar seasonal change *and/or* an emotional market turning point *or* a golden section division of a larger spiral.

- Spiral Calendar units that are evenly divisible by other natural time units are in *harmony* with those units and may have more pronounced or frequent effects on markets.

- Market turns that exhibit near Spiral Calendar measurement are in *approximation*.

CHAPTER 5

THE CAUSE OF PANICS AND CRASHES

AUTUMN FALLS

The predilection for market panics in the fall season is not a recent phenomenon. The panic of 1873 occurred on Friday, September 19. The opening paragraph in *The New York Times* the following day reported, "It is a singular coincidence that the gold corner of 1869, when so many were ruined, and the culmination of the panic of 1873, happened...in the same month." In this century, two major crashes, 1929 and 1987, as well as the mini-crash of 1989, occurred in October. There were also the "October Massacres" of 1978 and 1979. An examination of these five years in Spiral Calendar terms reveals a set of seasonal preconditions for October panics. I am only examining the years that contain a market top in October, which is followed by extreme weakness. Other years with sharp declines, including 1937, 1957 and 1990, were continuations of declines that began before October.

The fall season marks the end of the growing seasons of spring and summer and the onset of decay as life prepares for the hibernation of winter. Panics are a sharp transition from rising markets to declining markets, just as an early frost in the fall can be a sharp transition from summer to winter. Markets shedding prices and trees shedding leaves are natural expressions of the season. The seasons play a role in life, with spring and summer allied with growth and life, and fall and winter connected with decay and death. The seasons are not alone in aligning themselves on one side or the other of the growth–decay equation. I believe the new moon belongs with spring and summer as a positive life force. The full moon aligns with fall and winter as a manifestation of decay.

Year	New Moon following Spring Equinox	Days between	Market Highs	Lows	Days between	Full Moon following Winter Solstice
1929	4/1/27	924	10/11/29	10/29/29	1908	1/19/35
1978	3/30/76	926	10/12/78			
1979	3/19/77	930	10/5/79			
1987	3/21/85	925	10/2/87	10/20/87	1907	1/8/93
1989	3/29/87	926	10/10/89	10/16/89	1180	1/8/93
	average	926.2				
Equivalent Spiral Calendar periods in days:			927.6	1909.5		1180.1
Equivalent Spiral Calendar periods in years:			2½	5¼		3¼
Equivalent Spiral Calendar periods in moons:			$\sqrt{F_{16}}$	$\sqrt{F_{19}}$		$\sqrt{F_{17}}$

Table 5-1

The market peaks of 1929 and 1987 were within 24 hours of new moons, as was the 1720 mania peak. The 1946 emotional low and spiral focus was on the full moon. I am not suggesting that new moons are always price tops, or full moons price lows, just that these moon phases are each associated with one side of the growth–decay process.

The five years in the 20th century that saw October tops followed by extreme weakness belong in two categories. The panic years, 1929, 1987 and 1989, had distinct tops and bottoms sandwiching a period of price free fall. The massacre years, 1978 and 1979, had price tops preceding sharp declines. The massacre years did not contain the dramatic one day declines of the panic years. All five years have October tops made $\sqrt{F_{16}}$ moons from the spring equinox, new moon two and a half years earlier, with a variation of +2 to -4 days. The average distance from new moon, spring equinox to market top was 926.2 days, versus the Spiral Calendar 927.6 days. The three panic years made lows either $\sqrt{F_{17}}$ or $\sqrt{F_{19}}$ backwards from full moons following the winter solstice, with a variation of no more than three days. Table 5-1 contains the dates of the new moons two and a half years prior to the October tops, the distance from moon to top and the date of the top. For the panic years, the table shows the dates of the lows, the related full moon, winter solstice and the intervening Spiral Calendar period.

These three Spiral Calendar periods of 2½, 3¼ and 5¼ years contain *seasonal harmony*, that is, the time lengths are whole numbers of seasons as well as Spiral Calendar periods. *The half year increments forward from the spring and the quarter year increments backward from the winter collide in the fall*. See Figure 5-1.

In every panic and massacre year, the new moon two and a half years before the October top fell between one day before and ten days after the spring equinox. Conversely, there was a never a full moon in this time window. This is a precondition for an October slide to occur. This observation is important for forecasting. After the experiences of the late 1980s, everyone looks over their shoulder for the next October panic. Many forecasters predicted calamity for October 1991. Two and a half years earlier, the full moon fell two days after the spring equinox. The lunar-solar alignment prerequisite did not exist in 1991. The result, no panic that year.

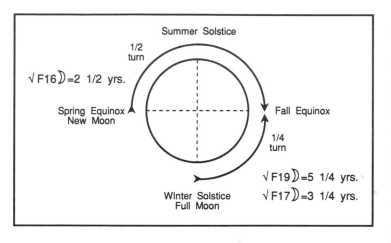

Figure 5-1

Figures 4-12 and 4-13 depict new moon, spring equinox spirals moving forward and creating October tops. Figures 4-8 and 4-10 show the full moon, winter solstice spirals moving backward to the lows. These are brought together in Figure 5-2, where we see the spiral geometry of the 1987 crash. These are the precise measurements and alignments that caused the extraordinary mass psychological panic. In any type of system or dynamic, it is during the extremes that an underlying structure becomes most apparent. Meteorologists crave the opportunity to have a full set of instruments in place at the vortex of a tornado, since so much would be learned about all types of weather. The crash is the market's version of the tornado. Here, the instruments of time, measured in lunar units of the square roots of the Fibonacci sequence, reveal the underlying structure with all the beauty, truth and precision of nature's other creations.

The diagram of the 1987 crash, Figure 5-2, illustrates a composite of the seasonal and Spiral Calendar components of the panic. The seasonal component requires the proper positioning of the lunar phase relative to the solar season for the panic effect to occur. Lunar and solar rhythms are not naturally synchronized. Sometimes they form harmonious relationships and other times not. It is the combination of these two separate beats with the geometry of the Spiral Calendar that determines the shape of the market's patterns. This point is best understood by studying examples of markets tracing nearly identical patterns at different times. These are analogies.

ANALOGIES

This book began by examining the similarity of 1929's trading pattern to 1987 in Figures 1-1 and 1-2. There is more to this similarity than the Spiral Calendar measurement of the intervening time period. Since this example, we have examined other market turns related by Spiral Calendar units, which do not possess the striking step by step similarity of the 1929 and 1987 charts. The 1929-1987 similarity qualifies it as an

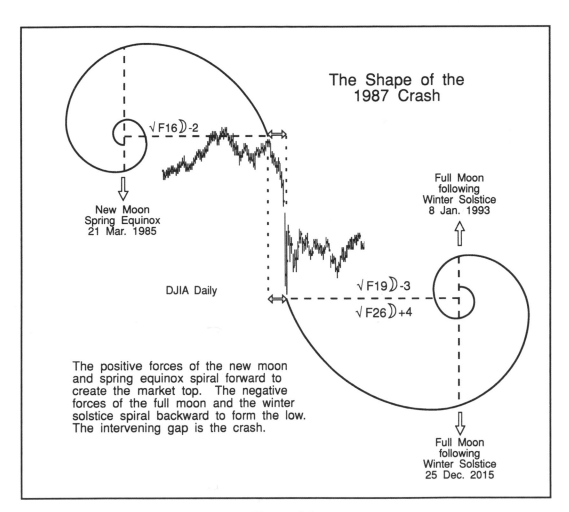

The Shape of the
1987 Crash

$\sqrt{F16}\!\!)\!-2$

New Moon
Spring Equinox
21 Mar. 1985

DJIA Daily

Full Moon
following
Winter Solstice
8 Jan. 1993

$\sqrt{F19}\!\!)\!-3$

$\sqrt{F26}\!\!)\!+4$

The positive forces of the new moon
and spring equinox spiral forward to
create the market top. The negative
forces of the full moon and the winter
solstice spiral backward to form the low.
The intervening gap is the crash.

Full Moon
following
Winter Solstice
25 Dec. 2015

Figure 5-2

analogy. The reason 1987 traced a nearly identical pattern to 1929 is harmony. The time unit that connects the years 1929 and 1987, $\sqrt{F29}$, contains lunar and solar harmony. Harmony means that the 1987 Spiral Calendar anniversaries of the comparable 1929 events occurred within ten days of the same time of year on the solar calendar, and within two days of the same lunar phase.

There are three known conditions necessary for an analogous market pattern to occur.

- The distance between the analogies must be a Spiral Calendar unit or the precise sum of more than one unit.

- The analogous markets occur at the same time of the year (solar harmony).

- The analogous markets occur at the same lunar phase (lunar harmony).

The 29th Spiral Calendar period *happen*s to be a whole number of solar years and lunar moons. This is the reason for the striking similarity of 1929 to 1987. Spiral

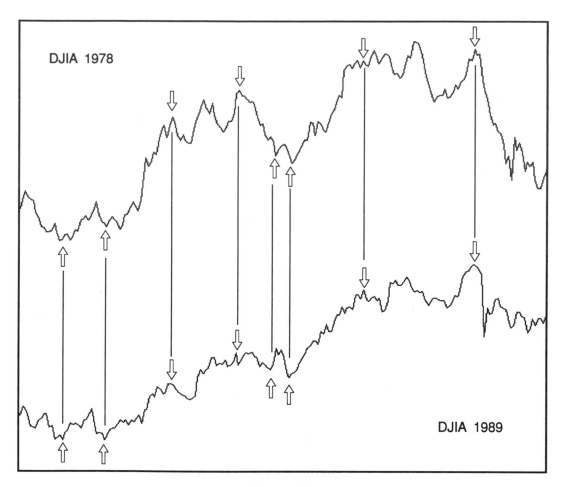

Figure 5-3

Calendar distances can connect market tops to bottoms and bottoms to tops; however, all examples of the 29th Spiral Calendar unit in this book connect the same type of market turn, i.e., bottom to bottom or top to top. This is the harmony of $\sqrt{F}_{29}$. All three calendar types, lunar, solar and spiral, which create the market's pattern, are in alignment. The other examples are 1799 to 1857, panic to panic, separated by $\sqrt{F}_{29}$, and 1884 to 1942, panic to low, also separated by $\sqrt{F}_{29}$. See Figure 4-3.

Figure 5-3 shows a market analogy not connected by $\sqrt{F}_{29}$, 1978 and 1989. These two years both saw double bottoms early in the year followed by sharp rises into double tops. Each market consolidated into two closely spaced lows followed by the sharpest rise of the year in early summer. Sideways consolidations marked by increasing volatility characterized the late summer and early autumn in both years. The final fall high in both cases fell near or on the Jewish lunar holy day of Yom Kippur. These tops are shown in Figures 4-13 and 4-14 with their respective spirals. The tops preceded the "October massacre" in 1978 and the "mini-crash" in 1989.

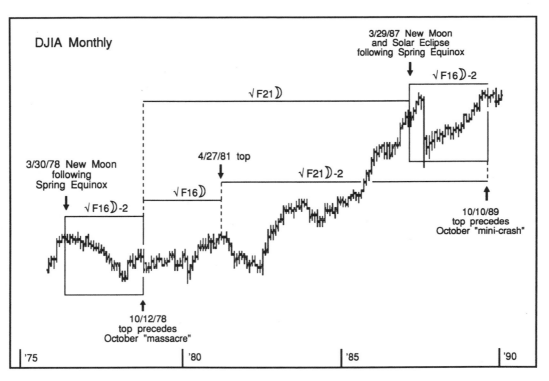

Figure 5-4

The time interval separating the 1978 and 1989 analogy, eleven years, is not a Spiral Calendar time period. Rather, it is the sum of two Spiral Calendar periods, $\sqrt{F}16$ and $\sqrt{F}21$ moons. The sum of these two particular periods are nearly whole numbers of moons and years. Those sums are 4017 days, or 136.04 moons (lunar harmony) and 10.998 years (solar harmony). The three conditions for analogous markets outlined above are met in the 1978-1989 example; the distance is a Spiral Calendar period or sum of periods, with solar harmony and lunar harmony in the intervening time length. Figure 5-4 shows that the point where the two Spiral Calendar periods ($\sqrt{F}16$ and $\sqrt{F}21$ moons) join is the April 27, 1981 high in the Dow Jones Industrial Average. This measurement is precisely $\sqrt{F}16$ moons forward from the October 1978 top and $\sqrt{F}21$ moons backwards less two days from the 1989 top.

The three preconditions for analogous markets are not the sole requirements for an analogy. After all, any two points in time separated by fifty-eight years will be a Spiral Calendar distance with lunar and solar harmony. The same is true for eleven years. Yet, the markets are not always tracing out the identical path of fifty-eight or eleven years ago. The differences are due to the larger structures of spirals and golden sections that govern the unfolding market patterns. *It is when those structures converge with the three analogy prerequisites that the "identical twin" analogies result.* In the 1929-1987 example, the relationship back from 1929 to 1835 is the evidence of a larger structure. Since the distance from 1835 to 1929 is $\sqrt{F}31$, a distance of $\sqrt{F}29$ (.618 times $\sqrt{F}31$) is a

1937 PEAK + 58 = 1995

69

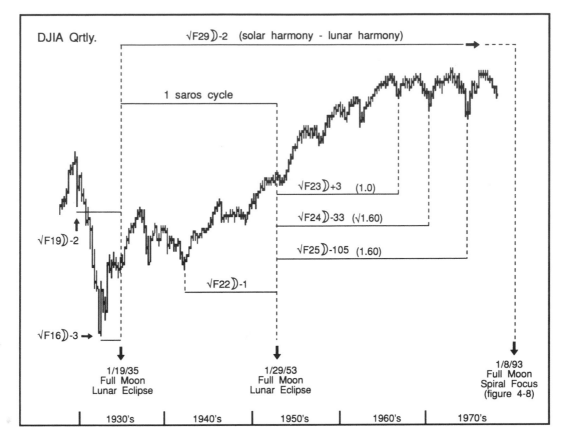

Figure 5-5

potential golden section. The top of 1981 serves the same purpose for the 1978-1989 analogy. The Spiral Calendar relationships indicating a larger framework are consistent with the periods that produced the analogies, $\sqrt{F_{29}}$ and $\sqrt{F_{16}} + \sqrt{F_{21}}$.

I have shown how the 1987 crash connects to the full moon, winter solstice focus of January 8, 1993. I have also shown how the 1987 crash connects to the 1929 crash by $\sqrt{F_{29}}$ moons, creating an analogy. Does the 1929 crash have a full moon, winter solstice focus? Are the foci for the two crashes themselves analogies connected by $\sqrt{F_{29}}$? Figure 5-5 shows that the full moon of January 19, 1935 is $\sqrt{F_{29}}$ moons minus two days from the January 8, 1993 focus and $\sqrt{F_{19}}$ moons minus two days from the 1929 crash. This moon is not the focus of a perfect spiral backwards on the odd Spiral Calendar sequence. It is, however, important as a focus for important market lows. The 16th Spiral Calendar period backwards from this full moon produced the low of July 8, 1932 with a precision of three days, as shown in Figure 5-5. This date is the lowest price for the Dow from 1907 to the present. The pattern produced by the full moon, winter solstice of January 19, 1935 is different from its 1993 counterpart, but the fact that it measures to the 1929 crash and the 1932 low is strong evidence for the negative aspects of full moons at winter solstices and their relationship to the Spiral Calendar.

The full moon of January 19, 1935 was also a lunar eclipse. Figure 5-5 shows the relevant Spiral Calendar relationships from the next lunar eclipse belonging to the same saros cycle, January 29, 1953. This eclipse measures forward to the October 1966 low (precise to 3 days) and backwards to the 1942 low (precise to 1 day). The January 1953 eclipse also relates, though only by *approximation,* to the lows of 1970 and 1974. The chart displays the near $\sqrt{\phi}$ proportions of the three lows forward from the lunar eclipse of January 1953.

The January full moons of 1935 and 1953 produced four precise and two approximate lows, as shown in Figure 5-5. Combine this with the perfect spirals of lows from full moons following winter solstices in 1993 and 2015 (Figures 4-8, 4-9, 4-10) and you can see that this lunar-solar combination is the negative force for market lows and October panics.

UNKIND MAY

After October, May is probably the most frequent month associated with sharp market slides and important lows. In recent market history, the low of May 26, 1970 is the most significant example of a May event. This low lies on the spiral backwards from the full moon, winter solstice of December 25, 2015, Figure 4-10.

Another year with a particularly nasty May for the stock market was 1940. This was the time of the German invasion of France. The Dow Jones Industrial Average for 1940, April through July, is shown in Figure 5-6.

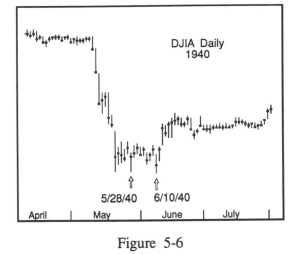

Figure 5-6

Two lows were made at the end of the market slide, the first on May 28 and the second on June 10. The second exceeded the first by only one tenth of a Dow point intra-day. Just as the October 1987 crash followed the May 1970 low by $\sqrt{F_{24}}$, so did a market low, October 1957, follow the May 1940 low by $\sqrt{F_{24}}$. Both the May 1940 and October 1957 lows measure backwards from the full moon following the winter solstice of December 27, 1985. The measurements in days between the two lows and the full moon are identical to the 1970 and 1987 example. The amount that each measurement varies from precision is exactly the same *to the day*, Figure 5-7. In each example, the distance from May to October low is $\sqrt{F_{24}}$ minus three days.

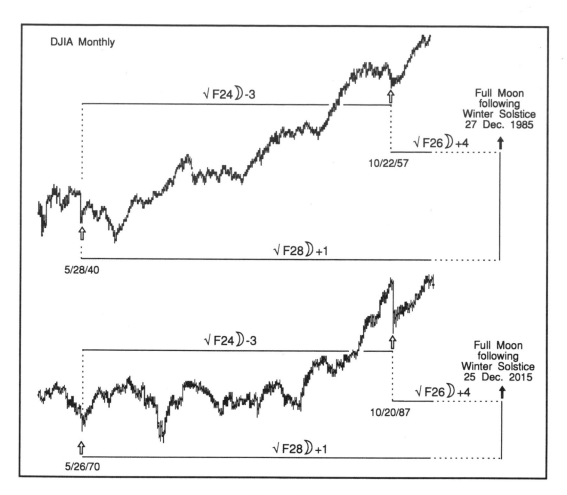

Figure 5-7

The low of June 10, 1940 is $\sqrt{F}14$ moons from the full moon following the winter solstice of January 2, 1942, shown in Figure 5-8. This spiral provides a good contrast to the perfect spiral of January 8, 1993, shown in Figure 4-8. The 1942 spiral moves backwards predominantly on the even sequence, in contrast to the odd sequence of the 1993 spiral. The 1942 example includes one turn on the odd sequence, and it skips one turn, $\sqrt{F}16$, on the even sequence. The 1942 spiral does not produce the same type of turns, all lows, as did the 1993 spiral, but rather a combination of highs and lows.

The 1942 focus measures to one other panic type low in addition to that of May 1940. January 2, 1942 minus $\sqrt{F}18$ moons precisely equals November 23, 1937, the low for that year and the autumn climax of a sharp drop. Figure 5-8 shows a second low on October 19, 1937 also measuring to a full moon following a winter solstice. This moon is January 13, 1941. The 1937 autumn drop was large and dramatic. Unlike the slides listed in Table 5-1, 1937 did not have a top in October preceding the decline. In that year, the market began its slide in August. The preconditions for market tops in October,

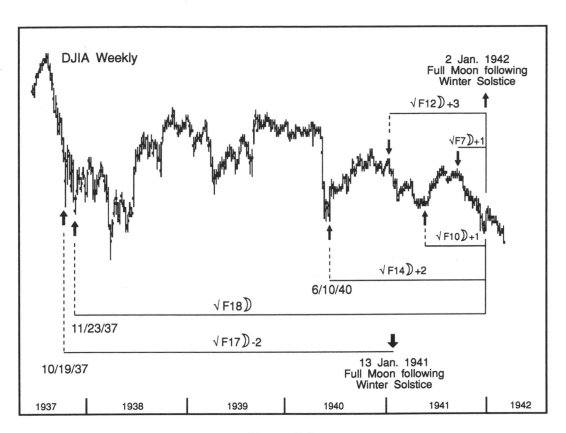

Figure 5-8

namely a new moon between the day before and ten days after the spring equinox 2½ years earlier, were not met in 1937. The spring new moon in 1935 fell 12 days after the equinox in 1935. The 1937 decline resembles 1987 in that *two* precise measurements to full moon, winter solstices figure in the formation of the market's lows.

PANIC SIGNATURES

A market in free fall will often trace a characteristic chart pattern, the *panic signature*. Five examples of this pattern in U.S. stock prices are assembled in Figure 5-9. Four of the five free fall drops lie on full moon, winter solstice spirals illustrated previously. The fifth, ending July 23, 1990, falls precisely on a golden section cut from the January 8, 1993 spiral. This point is marked in Figure 4-9. All five points are linked to adjacent points by the Spiral Calendar. Each link is precise within two days. The magnitude of each panic drop is perfectly consistent with its equivalent Spiral Calendar links to the other examples. The pattern for the 1929 and 1987 crashes is best seen in charts where each bar represents one week's trading. The 1989 mini-crash, linked by smaller Spiral Calendar sequences, displays the pattern on a smaller scale chart, daily bars. Still closer in time is the July 23, 1990 drop, which covered approximately 130 Dow points in three hours' time. The pattern here resembles the others when viewed on

73

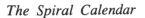

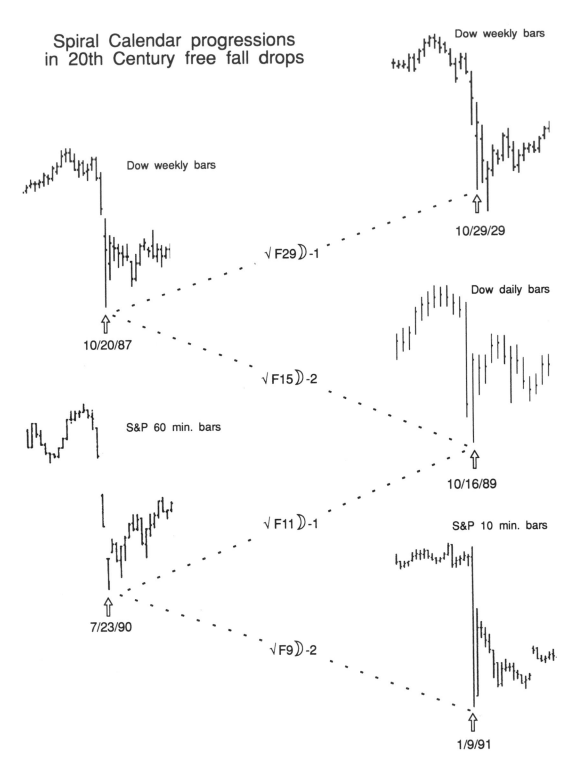

Figure 5-9

sixty minute bars. In the final example, the DJIA fell about 90 points in a few minutes on January 9, 1991. The Spiral Calendar sequence number linking January 9 to the previous drop is the smallest, as is the size of the market's drop in price and the time scale of the pattern, ten minute bars.

The free fall patterns are an example of *fractals*. Fractals are similar patterns that repeat in a variety of scales. Fractals appear naturally in living and non-living things.

Various fundamental causes are often ascribed to panics, only to have the next panic occur in the absence of those supposed causes. Market commentators usually try to blame panics on particular pieces of news, whether justifiably or not. Two of these five drops were actually concurrent with major news events of the time. The 1989 mini-crash was blamed on the collapse of the United Airlines takeover attempt, and the January 9, 1991 drop occurred on the news from Geneva of the failure for a peace breakthrough to avert the Gulf War. My argument for the Spiral Calendar over news as the cause of the drops is that the Spiral Calendar relationships appear in all five examples, while the news figured in only two instances. The truly convincing experience is to witness a market event forecasted using the Spiral Calendar occur on schedule. The next chapter will examine the forecasting methods to realize this end.

Market panics have long been considered a mystery. The original meaning of panic is "a sudden fear inspired by Pan," a reference to the Greek god. The Spiral Calendar lifts the veil of mystery from the bouts of sudden fear that periodically sweep the market. The five examples in Figure 5-9, which each contain the panic signature in their shape, are linked to each other and to the new moon, winter solstice by the Spiral Calendar. This is a dramatic and convincing demonstration of the Spiral Calendar's role as the time piece and primary regulator of social human nature. A later chapter will demonstrate that this timepiece tracks not only market behavior, but probably all emotional human history.

CHAPTER 6

FORECASTING METHODS

The best results from any forecasting method are realized when the capabilities and limitations of the method are understood. In the field of market forecasting, there is a history of searching for, and claiming to have found, "the holy grail," that method which will answer all questions and provide all knowledge regarding market direction and timing. I do not believe the Spiral Calendar is a "holy grail," or that one readily exists within our grasp. Rather, I liken the Spiral Calendar to the Rosetta Stone. The Rosetta Stone provided the key to translating Egyptian hieroglyphics. The Spiral Calendar provides the first *precise* translation between the scribbling of the market in the time dimension and the beats of nature's calendar. It must be remembered that while the Rosetta Stone answered age old questions about the Egyptians, by no means do we now know all there is about them. I expect the Spiral Calendar will ultimately raise nearly as many questions as it answers. The value, therefore, to the forecaster is in the use of the Spiral Calendar in conjunction with the other tools at his disposal. The Spiral Calendar, used correctly, will provide a tremendous advantage to those who invest their time in understanding its workings.

Success in investing or trading markets necessitates controlling the emotions of fear and greed. Lunacy is the appropriate word for mass emotion in markets. The Spiral Calendar's usefulness is its ability to pinpoint likely periods of market lunacy. This knowledge will allow you to avoid the pitfalls of lunacy in your own trading actions as well as profit from the lunacy of others.

The metaphor of waves on a lake is helpful in understanding the short term condition of markets the forecaster faces when using the Spiral Calendar. Waves are often a descriptor of market behavior. A moving boat on a smooth lake in the early morning makes a pattern of waves whose clarity resembles that of a single spiral. The source of each wave is as obvious as the focus of the spiral. In late afternoon, the lake fills with boats. The many intersecting waves combine with the wind to form a chop. The source of these choppy waves and their relationship to each other can seem impossible to understand. The source of the spirals (foci) and their interrelation is similar in markets.

Spiral Calendar analysis of short term time periods in markets reveals that market turns can relate by Spiral Calendar periods without necessarily lying on a recognizable spiral. Market turns will occur on points that measure from multiple previous turns using Spiral Calendar units. Precision and magnitude govern these relationships as on the more ordered spirals. These patterns may be golden sections, partial spirals or other fragmented structures.

This chapter contains the tools required for finding these structures, the techniques for discerning which structures will perform reliably and the unique trading strategies that derive from the forecasts.

TOOLS

The primary tool required for Spiral Calendar analysis is data. Because the output of the analysis is so precise, the data must also be precise. Precision in, precision out. Most analytic methods use monthly and yearly data for long term forecasts, weekly and daily for intermediate term and intra-day data for a short term time horizon. Spiral Calendar analysis always adds or subtracts in days, so daily data is required. I use hourly data, where available, for more exact results. The quantity of data will determine the scale of the resulting forecasts. Large amounts of daily data, sixty years plus, are needed to find the long term Spiral Calendar relationships that form the major, once-in-a-decade turns. Twenty to twenty-five years of daily data will substitute if the larger amounts are not available. Two to three years of data is sufficient for catching short term price swings, but it is unlikely you will catch the larger magnitude turns. There is no intra-day application of the Spiral Calendar, the shortest time period being twenty-nine days.

I use two tools to analyze the data, a computer spreadsheet to add or subtract Spiral Calendar units from past market turning points, and a hand calculator capable of performing date arithmetic. The computer can store large numbers of past turns and all the spiral computations deriving from them. Hand calculators usually have a larger built in calendar for adding and subtracting larger quantities of $\sqrt{F_n}$. The final tool I use is an ephemeris for finding the exact date and times of full and new moons in the past and future.

THE METHOD

The principal method for identifying potential market turning points is to add Spiral Calendar time periods to previous market turns. This approach will even identify the turns that seem to spiral back from the future, due to the additive nature of the sequence. A

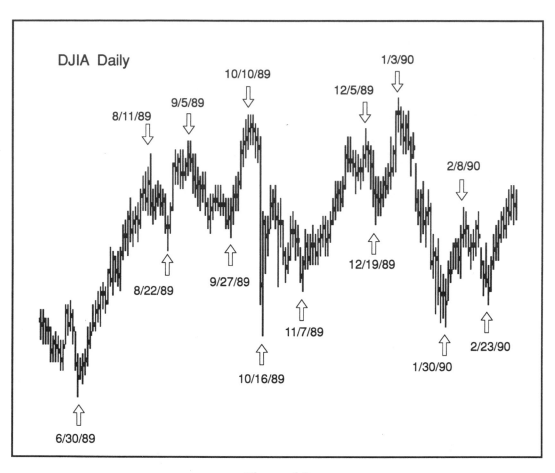

Figure 6-1

spreadsheet is ideal for this task. Figure 6-1 shows a section of the Dow Jones Industrial Average with the dates of the turns labeled. Table 6-1 is a spreadsheet constructed from those turns. The spreadsheet contains the previous market turns in the left column, headed by the name of the market under analysis. The other columns contain the date achieved by adding the Spiral Calendar sequence numbers, which are labeled in the top row. The spreadsheet indicates potential market turns when *two or more* projected dates in proximity form a *cluster*. Notice how the table produces the turns of the April 6, 1990 spiral shown in Figure 4-7.

    Examination of Table 6-1 shows many possible clusters of dates in proximity to each other. A selection criteria is necessary to determine what constitutes a cluster and which clusters will most reliably indicate emotional market extremes. The selection criteria reduce the number of possible clusters and increase the quality of the forecasts.

Dow	√f2	√f3	√f4	√f5	√f6	√f7	√f8	√f9
6/30/89	7/30/89	8/11/89	8/20/89	9/4/89	9/22/89	10/14/89	11/12/89	12/19/89
8/11/89	9/10/89	9/22/89	10/1/89	10/16/89	11/3/89	11/25/89	12/24/89	1/30/90
8/22/89	9/21/89	10/3/89	10/12/89	10/27/89	11/14/89	12/6/89	1/4/90	2/10/90
9/5/89	10/5/89	10/17/89	10/26/89	11/10/89	11/28/89	12/20/89	1/18/90	2/24/90
9/27/89	10/27/89	11/8/89	11/17/89	12/2/89	12/20/89	1/12/90	2/9/90	3/18/90
10/10/89	11/9/89	11/21/89	11/30/89	12/15/89	1/2/90	1/24/90	2/22/90	3/31/90
10/16/89	11/14/89	11/27/89	12/6/89	12/21/89	1/7/90	1/30/90	2/28/90	4/6/90
11/7/89	12/6/89	12/19/89	12/28/89	1/12/90	1/29/90	2/21/90	3/22/90	4/28/90
12/5/89	1/4/90	1/16/90	1/25/90	2/9/90	2/27/90	3/21/90	4/19/90	5/26/90
12/19/89	1/17/90	1/30/90	2/8/90	2/23/90	3/12/90	4/4/90	5/3/90	6/9/90
1/3/90	2/2/90	2/14/90	2/23/90	3/10/90	3/28/90	4/19/90	5/18/90	6/24/90
1/30/90	3/1/90	3/13/90	3/22/90	4/6/90	4/24/90	5/17/90	6/14/90	7/21/90
2/8/90	3/10/90	3/22/90	3/31/90	4/15/90	5/3/90	5/25/90	6/23/90	7/30/90
2/23/90	3/25/90	4/6/90	4/15/90	4/30/90	5/18/90	6/9/90	7/8/90	8/14/90

Table 6-1

CRITERIA

Consistency in *magnitude* should determine the selection of previous market turns to input. Important turns in the past will produce important turns in the future when connected by large sequence numbers. Smaller turns will connect with smaller turns by small sequence numbers. The quantity of data and the resolution of the market you desire dictate the selection of relevant past market points. There will always be some subjectivity in applying this idea. The analyst must be careful since, at the smaller sequence numbers, inputting too many previous turns will result in far too many clusters. The goal is not to find every minute trend change, but rather to find a few high probability opportunities for profit. I look for previous turns at which the market makes a change of emotional *character*. Such changes usually coincide with trend changes.

What constitutes a cluster? *A cluster consists of two or more dates in proximity.* The definition of proximity is relative to the sequence numbers that produce the clusters. The Spiral Calendar contains two additive sequences, the odd sequence numbers and the even sequence numbers. *Projected dates that lie on <u>the same additive sequence</u>, odd or even, produce the highest quality forecasts.* These clusters have two, four, six or eight, as the difference of their sequence numbers. The ratio of the longer distance to the shorter will be among the ratios of Table 3-2: 1.618, 2.618, 4.236, etc. *Projected dates will be in proximity if they differ by no more than six calendar days and they are on the same additive sequence.*

Clusters on *different additive sequences* will have an odd number (1, 3 or 5) as the difference between sequence numbers. Such clusters will not produce forecasts as reliable as those on the same additive sequence. Stricter proximity requirements are used for different additive sequence clusters to improve the quality of the forecasts. *Dates on different additive sequences must differ by no more than three calendar days to be proximate.* Clusters should also be defined by the difference in their sequence numbers. If this number is too large, the difference in magnitudes is too great and the forecast components lose relative proportion. Eight and five are good limits for the sequence number differential for same and different sequences respectively. The cluster parameters are summarized in Table 6-2.

Cluster Parameters		
	Same Sequence (odd and odd, even and even)	Different Sequence (odd and even)
Calendar Day Difference	6 days or less	3 days or less
Sequence Number Difference	8 or less	5 or less

Table 6-2

The purpose of these guidelines is not to determine what does or does not belong to a spiral or like structure. Certain points on a spiral will lie outside this definition of precision. The purpose is to set parameters for a disciplined trading approach.

The parameters that define clusters will determine how much precision to require in the forecasts. Each projected date in a cluster implies a "time frame" when a market turn would be precise. I insist on each turn occurring no more than three calendar days from each projected date in the cluster. This constraint makes the time frame associated with each date seven days wide, the date itself plus three days on each side.

The *time frames* of the projected dates in the cluster generate the *time window. The time window is the overlap of the time frames from two or more dates in the cluster. The time window is the location of the expected turn.* By definition, the time window will be no more than seven calendar days or five trading days wide. These are tight parameters, especially when forecasting turns of large magnitude. Figure 6-2 illustrates these concepts. The larger the space between dates in the cluster, the smaller the overlap of the time frames, hence the smaller acceptable time window. This is a logical constraint as the larger cluster appears sloppy and must meet stricter requirements to maintain *precision.* A cluster separated by six days will have only a one day time window, while a cluster of two or more days on the same date will have a time window five trading days wide. You will *always* be looking for a turn *within three days of two projected Spiral Calendar dates.*

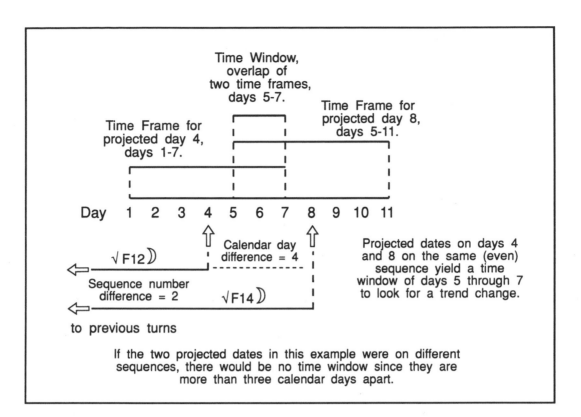

Figure 6-2

What should you look for in time windows? Turns most often occur at the center of the time window. Among relationships on the same additive sequence, golden sections seem to produce the best results. Golden sections occur when the difference of the sequence numbers is two (ratio .618) or four (ratio .382), expanding or contracting respectively. A golden section relationship when both previous turns are the same type, i.e., highs or lows, will usually produce the same type of turn again. The type of resulting turn is not consistently predictable when the previous turns are not the same type or the cluster lies on different additive sequences.

More than two projected dates can form a cluster or two close clusters. I call this a large cluster. If a large cluster occurs near a lunar phase and equinox or solstice, then the point is probably a focus. If not, look for a trend change at that point. If the structure indicates two separate time windows close together, the turn could occur in either one. The largest sequence number will likely indicate the magnitude of the turn even when it occurs in the time window formed from the smaller sequences. When many projected dates are close together, it is possible that some will forecast a turn while others do not. A time window comprising all the projected dates may not be accurate, while a time window containing some of the dates may be precise. This can be tricky to forecast. Close observation of the emotional character of the market is best for helping pinpoint the expected turn. I will expand upon these points in the examples.

When a large cluster indicates a potential focus, the center of the time window can be used as a point from which to subtract Spiral Calendar periods to find additional turning points. An example of this is shown for the Japanese stock market in the next chapter.

If a market *advances into a cluster near a new moon or declines into a cluster near a full moon*, look for the trend change on the moon phase. This is the *only time* to look for trend changes on specific moon phases. Markets can produce double tops or bottoms when one of the turns is in the time window and the other is just before or after the time window. The turn outside the time window may have the more extreme price of the two, but the price differential should not be significant.

SENTIMENT & THE WAVE PRINCIPLE

Any method of technical analysis will work best when integrated with other proven methods. My primary concern is with one indicator, the Spiral Calendar, not with constructing the ideal trading system from many indicators. However, two methods of technical analysis integrate well with the Spiral Calendar, market sentiment and the Wave Principle. The purpose of this book is to provide original research. Consequently, a detailed discussion of these methods is not appropriate here.

Sentiment indicators measure emotions, which reach extremes coincident with price extremes in markets. Rational expectations and attitudes give way to rationalization, which support predetermined emotional opinions. Spiral Calendar relationships coincide with price extremes. Identifying Spiral Calendar relationships and sentiment extremes together increases the ability to catch price extremes.

I place sentiment indicators into two categories, those which show where people have put their money and those which are polls of people's opinions. I trust the indicators more that are based on actions as opposed to opinions, although both types have compiled good track records. For the stock market, popular action indicators include option put/call ratios, which measure bullish and bearish exposure among option traders. Mutual fund cash ratios measure the money available as buying power to the large commercial funds. The Arms index created by Richard Arms, also known as the "trading index," measures the proportion of stock volume in the advancing stocks versus the declining stocks. For commodities, open interest and the commitment of traders reports can highlight which sides of the market the money is moving into and out of. Opinion indicators include various polls of traders, investors and investment advisors.

Sentiment indicators work because, at extremes, they point to instances where so many people are on one side of the market that no new traders can be found to continue the move. The trend is untenable. There will always be more buyers than sellers at tops and more sellers than buyers at bottoms. That will never change. Specific indicators may lose their ability to measure the quantity of buyers and sellers, but the principle of sentiment indicators will always be sound. Sentiment indicators are the best tools for confirming the excess of emotion found at market turns that coincide with Spiral Calendar turning points.

The Elliott Wave Principle first recognized φ in the patterns and prices of the market. This is an excellent complement to the Spiral Calendar, which applies φ to the time dimension. The best starting point for further research is Frost and Prechter's *Elliott Wave Principle*. I will present an example of a φ price relationship in Chapter 7.

TRADING TECHNIQUES

Effective trading of Spiral Calendar clusters requires:

- that the cluster's potential to produce a change in trend is confirmed by market action, i.e. extreme market behavior and/or sentiment lunacy at the time of the indicated turn or an extreme change in market character immediately after the indicated cluster.

- a disciplined entry and exit trading strategy that capitalizes on the precision of the Spiral Calendar to limit losses.

The Spiral Calendar presents opportunities to devise unique trading strategies that reduce risk and increase profit. Precision and magnitude combine to give the trader *perspective* from which current market behavior can be judged.

Trading systems that purport to generate turning points will often generate two or three points per week without an indication of which points are more important. Effective use of the Spiral Calendar will usually produce zero to three points per month. Evaluate these points for precision, magnitude and additive sequence structure to find the most important. With these points in mind, you should then monitor market behavior for increases in emotion and lunacy into the various turn points. A perception of the condition of other market indicators helps in making a trading decision. Traders are consistently premature in their buying. The knowledge of the location of large magnitude clusters enables the formulation of longer term outlooks. For example, suppose a lengthy bear market shows all the signs of imminently ending. The Spiral Calendar shows a tremendous large magnitude perfect spiral low due in 3 months. This invaluable market perspective enables the trader to exercise great patience.

I have two trading approaches which utilize the Spiral Calendar, conservative and aggressive. The conservative trader acts after the market turns in the time window. This eliminates many false signals and improves the percentage of profitable trades. The aggressive approach anticipates the potential turn and achieves better entry pricing on trades. Let me outline the tremendous advantage the Spiral Calendar affords both methods. The examples that follow in this chapter will show many instances of major turns in time windows that precede market moves of several weeks, months or years. When the resulting move is of great duration, the profits relative to the entry risk are substantial. Conventional analytical

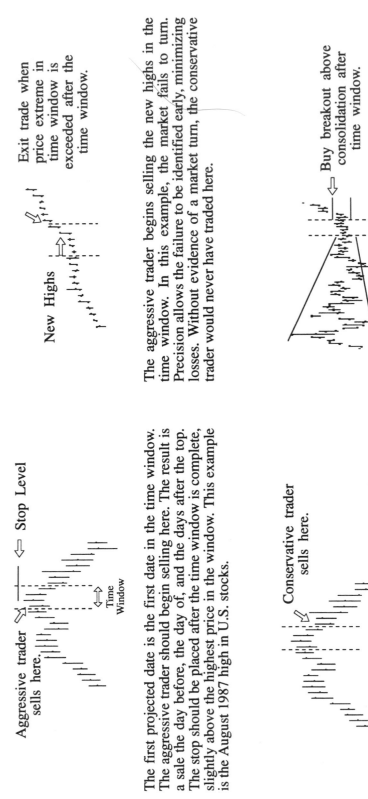

New Highs

Exit trade when price extreme in time window is exceeded after the time window.

The aggressive trader begins selling the new highs in the time window. In this example, the market fails to turn. Precision allows the failure to be identified early, minimizing losses. Without evidence of a market turn, the conservative trader would never have traded here.

Aggressive trader sells here. ⇩ Stop Level

Time Window

The first projected date is the first date in the time window. The aggressive trader should begin selling here. The result is a sale the day before, the day of, and the days after the top. The stop should be placed after the time window is complete, slightly above the highest price in the window. This example is the August 1987 high in U.S. stocks.

Conservative trader sells here.

The conservative trader will sell after the completion of the time window only if there is evidence of a turn in the time window. The conservative trader will not obtain as favorable a price as the aggressive trader. The stop level for the trade is the same as for the aggressive trader, but since the trade is not entered until the completion of the time window, the stop level is known at the time the trade is entered.

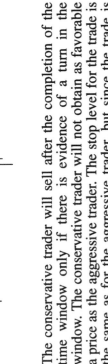

Buy breakout above consolidation after time window.

When the market consolidates into a time window, the aggressive trader can position to buy or sell a sharp move during or immediately after the time window. Here the trader would have bought gold in late November 1979 prior to the price doubling in eight weeks. Conservative traders should not trade markets that lack direction into time windows.

Figure 6-3

84

techniques require relatively large stop levels (the price to exit the trade and cut losses or preserve profits). Timing precision allows you to trade the larger moves with the tight stops normally reserved for short term trading. The advantage is getting the long term answers, right or wrong, in a short term time frame. If wrong on the turn, you can minimize price risk tremendously.

The conservative approach first requires the market to trend decisively into the time window. The conservative trader waits for evidence of a turn before acting. The conservative trader shouldn't trade a market that lacks a trend or meanders into the time window. Look for evidence of lunacy in sentiment indicators when possible. If the market appears to turn, enter the trade after the time window is over. If the market makes a dramatic turn in the time window, it is prudent to trade during the time window. The conservative trader misses the first days and points of a move. This is a small sacrifice in return for a significant advantage. Place the stop just above the extreme high price or just below the extreme low price in the time window. Allow for a slight new price extreme after the time window, but never tolerate significant losses.

The aggressive approach allows trading into a trend when that trade makes new price extremes in the time window and meets one of three conditions: the market reaches the first projected date *in* the time window; the market evidences a turn in the time window; or the market reaches the midpoint of the time window. The advantage to the aggressive approach is that the price of the trade will be extremely close to the extreme of the move in the successful trades. In addition, being a little early in a trade can allow for more favorable execution of a trade. It's easier to sell in quantity when there are many buyers before a top than immediately after when the buyers have been exhausted. The aggressive approach can trade markets that move sideways into a time window. In this situation, look for a dramatic move out of the consolidation pattern. Figure 6-3 displays the trading techniques.

THE EXAMPLES

The examples below discuss three different markets, U.S. stocks, U.S. bond futures and gold futures. Chapter 7 discusses the Japanese stock market. The method may be applied to any widely followed market. Emotional markets provide the best results. The Spiral Calendar does not appear to suit agricultural markets, which exhibit strong evidence of adherence to cycles based on their own crop life rhythms.

The bond and gold data in the examples use the day of the price extremes and add the Spiral Calendar unit rounded to the nearest day. The stock examples use the hourly price extremes and add the Spiral Calendar units including the fraction of the day for a more accurate projection. The results are rounded to the day. Each example shows the spreadsheet calculation, a chart of the relationships and outcome, plus commentary.

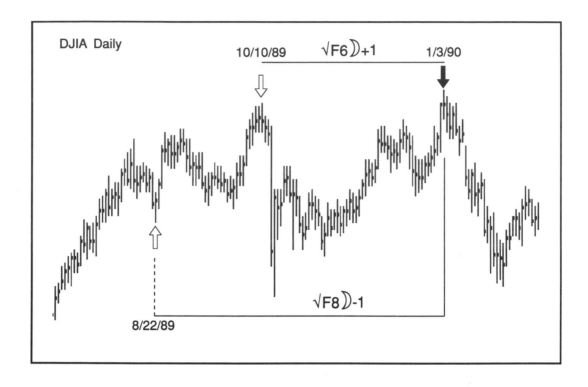

Dow		$\sqrt{f6}$	$\sqrt{f7}$	$\sqrt{f8}$
8/22/89		11/14/89	12/6/89	1/4/90
10/10/89		1/2/90	1/24/90	2/22/90

EXAMPLE 1

This first example from the Dow Jones Industrial Average forms a golden section. The middle point of the three proportions divides the entire length into a golden section. The projected dates on the spreadsheet are January 2, 1990, which is $\sqrt{F6}$ moons from the October 10, 1989 high, and January 4, 1990, which is $\sqrt{F8}$ moons from the August 22, 1989 low. The shorter length is .618 times the longer. This is an expanding golden section. The distance from the October top to the January top is greater than the distance from the August low to the October top. The pattern is expanding across time. Expanding golden sections exist when the difference in the sequence numbers is two. The market top of January 3 fell exactly between the two projected dates and led to a sharp one month decline. Notice on this and the subsequent examples how the resulting turns are similar in magnitude to the previous turns to which they relate. There is a relative proportion to the turns which over time you will begin to see as *natural*.

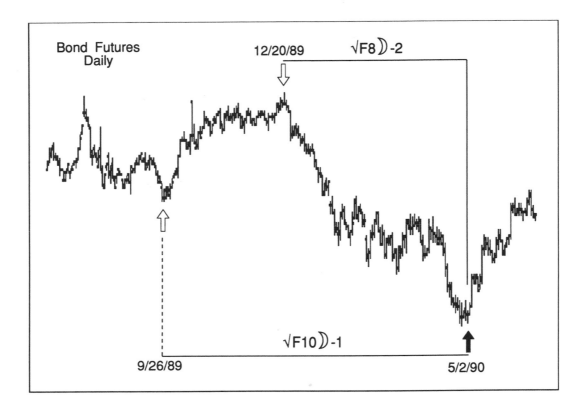

Bonds		$\sqrt{f8}$	$\sqrt{f9}$	$\sqrt{f10}$
9/26/89		2/8/90	3/17/90	5/3/90
12/20/89		5/4/90	6/10/90	7/27/90

Example 2

This example in bonds is another expanding golden section. The projected dates are May 3 and 4, 1990. The low price occurred on Friday, April 27, before the beginning of the time window on Tuesday, May 1. On May 2, inside the time window, prices came back down to within three ticks of the low. They then reversed to begin an extended rally. This is a very tradable situation. A trader waiting for the evidence of the turn still has plenty of market move to profit from. The sharp turn in the time window indicates the importance of the cluster of dates. The fact that the price extreme is outside the window by two trading days and three price ticks does not invalidate the cluster because of the sharp turn that occurs within the time window.

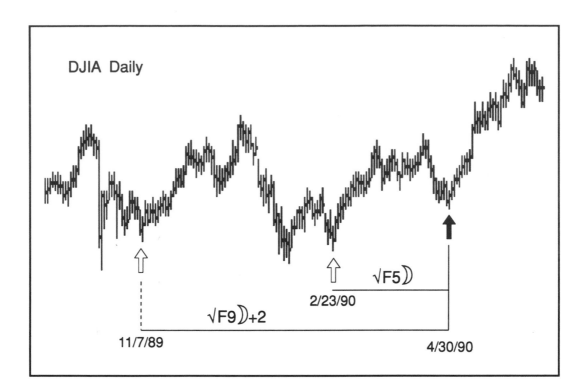

Dow		√ƒ5	√ƒ6	√ƒ7	√ƒ8	√ƒ9
11/7/89		1/12/90	1/29/90	2/21/90	3/22/90	4/28/90
2/23/90		4/30/90	5/18/90	6/9/90	7/8/90	8/14/90

EXAMPLE 3

The third example is a contracting golden section in the DJIA. The sequence numbers differ by four. The shorter distance is .382 the longer. The projected dates are two days apart, April 28 and 30. The time window is from April 27 (30 minus 3) to May 1 (28 plus 3). The 28th and 29th are on the weekend, making the time window three trading days wide. Unlike the first two examples, here the types of previous turns are the same, market lows. This situation indicates that a low is expected because it is a golden section. The market traded decisively down into the time window and made its low precisely on the second projected date. A sharp and profitable rally ensued.

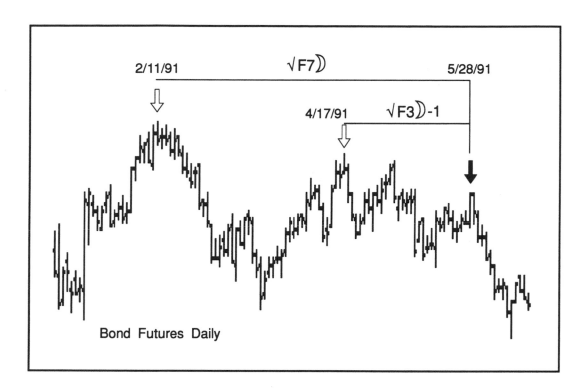

Bond Futures Daily

Bonds		√$f3$	√$f4$	√$f5$	√$f6$	√$f7$
2/11/91		3/25/91	4/3/91	4/18/91	5/6/91	5/28/91
4/17/91		5/29/91	6/7/91	6/22/91	7/10/91	8/1/91

EXAMPLE 4

Here is another contracting golden section. The previous turns are market highs, resulting in a high in the time window. The precision is excellent. The magnitude of the move into and out of the time window is relatively small, but so are the previous turns and the sequence numbers that form the golden section.

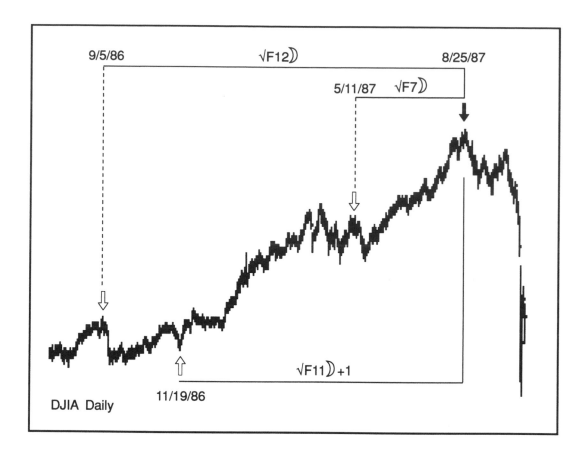

Dow		$\sqrt{f7}$	$\sqrt{f8}$	$\sqrt{f9}$	$\sqrt{f10}$	$\sqrt{f11}$	$\sqrt{f12}$
9/5/86		12/20/86	1/18/87	2/24/87	4/12/87	6/10/87	8/25/87
11/19/86		3/5/87	4/3/87	5/10/87	6/26/87	8/24/87	11/8/87
5/11/87		8/25/87	9/23/87	10/30/87	12/16/87	2/14/88	4/30/88

EXAMPLE 5

This next examples are golden sections where a third projected date on the other additive sequence confirms the cluster. The example is the Dow in August 1987, when three projected dates cluster on August 24 and 25. If you had data from 1929, a fourth projected date would be on the spreadsheet, August 24, from the 9/3/1929 top. The golden section comprises sequence numbers $\sqrt{F_7}$ and $\sqrt{F_{11}}$. The top on September 5, 1986 measures $\sqrt{F_{12}}$ to August 25. This supports the golden section's case for a turn here. $\sqrt{F_{12}}$ is an even number of moons, twelve, which produces lunar harmony. It will generate the same type of turn most of the time. Here they are both tops. Figure 6-3 shows the time window for this example in detail. The DJIA high for 1987 was August 25.

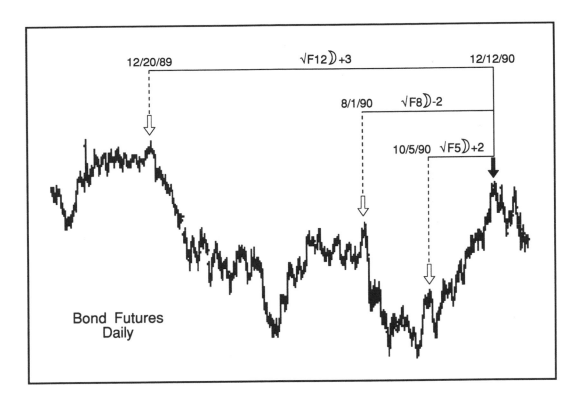

Bonds		√*f*5		√*f*8	√*f*9	√*f*10	√*f*11	√*f*12
12/20/89		2/24/90		5/4/90	6/10/90	7/27/90	9/25/90	12/9/90
8/1/90		10/6/90		12/14/90	1/20/91	3/8/91	5/7/91	7/21/91
10/5/90		12/10/90		2/17/91	3/26/91	5/12/91	7/11/91	9/24/91

EXAMPLE 6

This golden section in bonds on the even sequence is joined by a third projected date on the odd sequence. The three previous turns and the resulting turn are tops. The projected dates in the golden section differ by five days. This makes the time window only two days wide, December 11 and 12. Any other dates would be four or more days from one of the two projected dates. The resulting top of December 12 meets the precision criteria for all three projected dates.

91

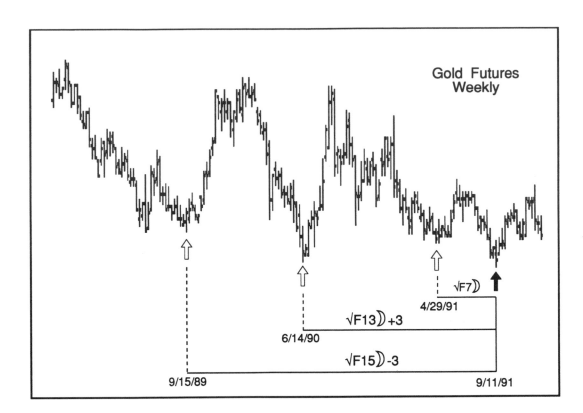

Gold		$\sqrt{f}8$		$\sqrt{f}13$	$\sqrt{f}14$	$\sqrt{f}15$
9/15/89		1/28/90		12/10/90	4/11/91	9/14/91
6/14/90		10/27/90		9/8/91	1/8/92	6/12/92
4/29/91		9/11/91		7/23/92	11/22/92	4/27/93

EXAMPLE 7

The September 1991 low in gold was the result of an expanding golden section. The projected dates differ by six days, the maximum allowed by the guidelines. By itself, that fact does not indicate a strong relationship, but combined with the following facts, the picture changes. This is a golden section, the most reliable of Spiral Calendar formations. The previous turns are of large magnitude. Each was the price low in its respective year, 1989 and 1990. The sequence numbers are significantly large. The $\sqrt{F}15$ moons is two years in length, producing solar harmony. The six day difference in projected dates results in a one day time window. This date, September 11, is confirmed by a projection from another low, April 29, 1991. The result of these three previous lows is that the low for 1991 was made on September 11, 1991, exactly on the one day time window.

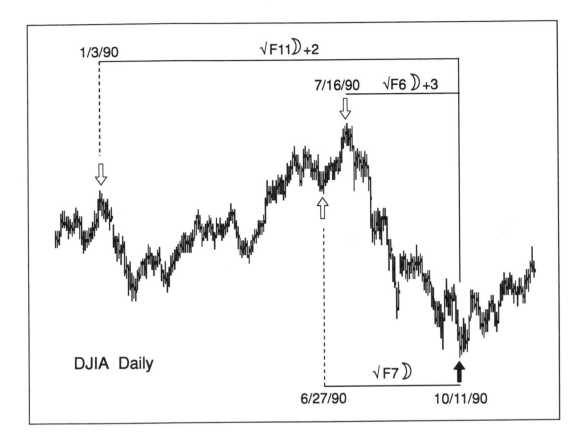

Dow		$\sqrt{f6}$	$\sqrt{f7}$	$\sqrt{f8}$	$\sqrt{f9}$	$\sqrt{f10}$	$\sqrt{f11}$
1/3/90		3/28/90	4/19/90	5/18/90	6/24/90	8/10/90	10/9/90
6/27/90		9/18/90	10/11/90	11/9/90	12/16/90	2/1/91	4/2/91
7/16/90		10/8/90	10/31/90	11/28/90	1/4/91	2/20/91	4/21/91

EXAMPLE 8

This is the final example of a golden section supplemented with a third projected date. Here the time window is October 8 through 11, 1990 for the Dow Jones Industrial Average. The price low occurred on the final day of the time window. A trader using the aggressive approach would not have bought until the day of the low, as the market had not made price extremes until then. Notice the comparable magnitude of the turns involved. The July 16 top and the October 11 low were the high and low price extremes for 1990.

93

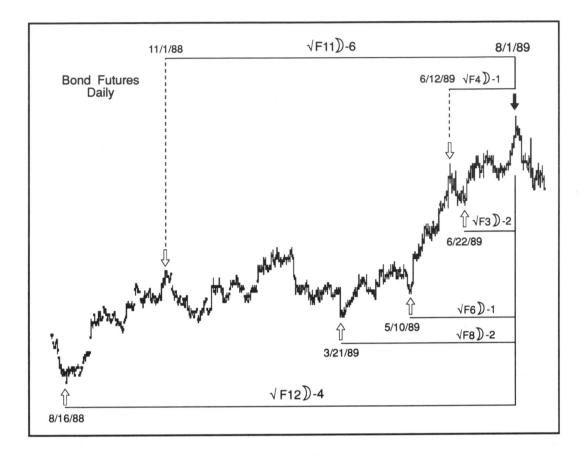

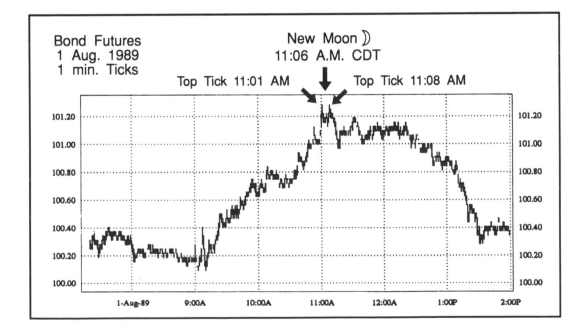

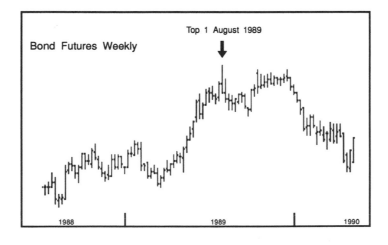

EXAMPLE 9

The next sets of examples are large clusters, four or more projected dates that form one or more time windows close together. In 1989, six turns in U.S. bond futures projected dates from August 2 through 5. The previous turns were both highs and lows and measured from the odd and even additive sequences. Bonds were in a long term uptrend, which accelerated as the date of the cluster approached. The new moon occurred during trading on August 1, the day before the first projected date. The top came dramatically on August 1. Bonds were up sharply that day. They reached their high five minutes before the exact time of the new moon. Prices backed off slightly before returning to the high seven minutes later, two minutes after the new moon. The advance could not be sustained, and bonds ended the day down sharply, with the bulls routed. The one minute tick chart shows the uncanny precision with which the new moon marked the top. The weekly chart shows the large magnitude of the turn. Bonds declined for a year and did not exceed the August 1, 1989 price for over two years. Notice the extreme similarity in the shapes of the one minute chart and the weekly chart. They are a good example of fractals of very different scales.

Bonds	$\sqrt{f}3$	$\sqrt{f}4$	$\sqrt{f}6$	$\sqrt{f}8$	$\sqrt{f}11$	$\sqrt{f}12$
8/16/88	9/27/88	10/6/88	11/8/88	12/29/88	5/22/89	8/5/89
11/1/88	12/13/88	12/22/88	1/24/89	3/16/89	8/7/89	10/21/89
3/21/89	5/2/89	5/11/89	6/13/89	8/3/89	12/25/89	3/10/90
5/10/89	6/21/89	6/30/89	8/2/89	9/22/89	2/13/90	4/29/90
6/12/89	7/24/89	8/2/89	9/4/89	10/25/89	3/18/90	6/1/90
6/22/89	8/3/89	8/12/89	9/14/89	11/4/89	3/28/90	6/11/90

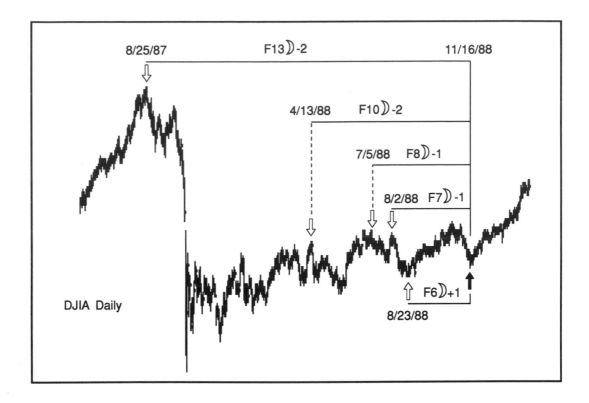

Dow		√f6	√f7	√f8	√f9	√f10		√f13
8/25/87		11/17/87	12/10/87	1/7/88	2/13/88	3/31/88		11/18/88
4/13/88		7/5/88	7/28/88	8/26/88	10/2/88	11/18/88		7/8/89
7/5/88		9/27/88	10/20/88	11/17/88	12/24/88	2/9/89		9/29/89
8/2/88		10/25/88	11/17/88	12/15/88	1/21/89	3/9/89		10/27/89
8/23/88		11/15/88	12/8/88	1/5/89	2/11/89	3/30/89		11/17/89

EXAMPLE 10

This large cluster is for the DJIA. Five projected dates form a time window between November 15 and 18, 1988. The largest sequence number, √F13, connects to the August 1987 high. The market low occurred on November 16, the second day of the four day time window. This low was an excellent example of the power of using sentiment to confirm market turns. In mid-November 1988, put/call ratios, trading index and advisor sentiment all reached extremes seen only at important market bottoms.

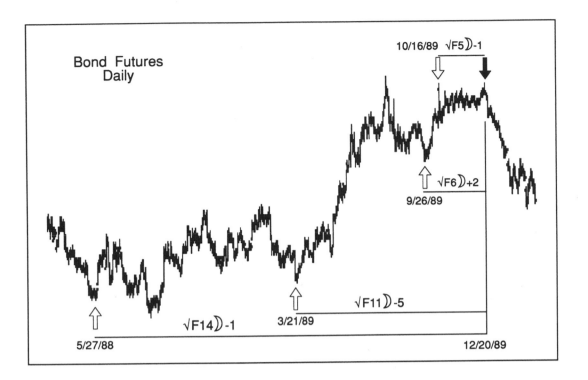

Bonds	$\sqrt{f}5$	$\sqrt{f}6$	$\sqrt{f}11$	$\sqrt{f}12$	$\sqrt{f}13$	$\sqrt{f}14$
5/27/88	8/1/88	8/19/88	3/2/89	5/16/89	8/21/89	12/21/89
3/21/89	5/26/89	6/13/89	12/25/89	3/10/90	6/15/90	10/15/90
9/26/89	12/1/89	12/19/89	7/2/90	9/15/90	12/21/90	4/22/91
10/16/89	12/21/89	1/8/90	7/22/90	10/5/90	1/10/91	5/12/91

EXAMPLE 11

This next large cluster occurred in bonds in 1989. All four dates cannot form one time window, as the projected dates $\sqrt{F}6$, December 19, and $\sqrt{F}11$, December 25, are separated by 6 calendar days, too far apart for dates on the different, odd and even, sequences. Excluding $\sqrt{F}11$, the time window for the other three dates is Monday, December 18 through Friday, December 22. The top fell on December 20. When a large cluster of dates contains some that are less precise than others, look for the turn to occur nearer the precise clustering, but consider the other dates as confirmation of the magnitude and validity of the turn. The August 5 and 7 date projections in Example 9 serve the same purpose.

97

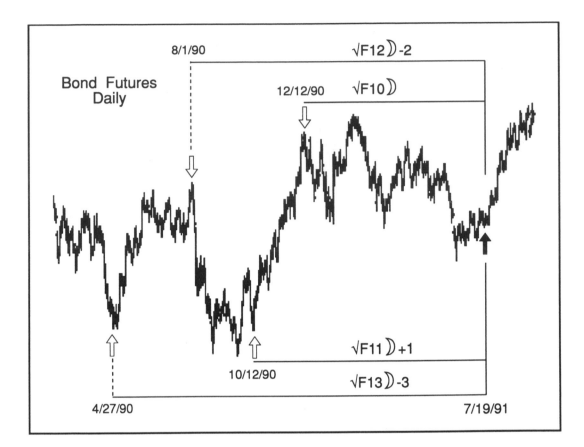

Bonds		√f10	√f11	√f12	√f13
4/27/90		12/2/90	1/31/91	4/16/91	7/22/91
8/1/90		3/8/91	5/7/91	7/21/91	10/26/91
10/12/90		5/19/91	7/18/91	10/1/91	1/6/92
12/12/90		7/19/91	9/17/91	12/1/91	3/7/92

EXAMPLE 12

Four previous turns in bonds formed a cluster of projected dates within five calendar days in July 1991. The chart shows these as two golden sections, one of highs on the even additive sequence and one of lows on the odd additive sequence. Normally, you should expect each golden section to produce the same type of turn as its previous turns. The market bore out this apparent duel of topping and bottoming forces by forming a consolidation into the time window. The odd sequence lows contain the larger sequence numbers, and those lows are of larger magnitude. The net distance the market traveled from the lows is greater than from the highs. This fact implies that the result of the consolidation should be a low.

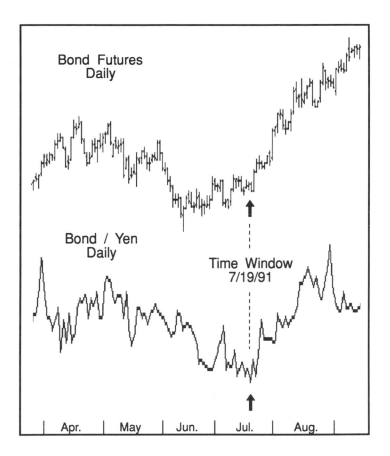

The market resolved to the upside following the time window. The move out of the consolidation exhibited the expected dramatic change in character, including an increase in volume.

How a market behaves at the indicated cluster is critical to determining the correct trading strategy. This book concentrates on the time dimension of market behavior, but price action also needs to be monitored closely. Price is money, and the definition of money is itself always fluctuating. The chart above shows the time window for bonds as well as the bond/ Japanese yen ratio. This is the price as it would appear to someone in Japan who was trading bonds, taking into account the currency fluctuations of the yen versus the dollar. The chart shows that by changing how we define money, the price action is different. In yen terms, bonds bottomed exactly in the time window. The new price lows of the bond/yen ratio, combined with the dramatic emotional change in the market after the time window confirm, the validity of the Spiral Calendar clusters. The globalization of all markets and the intentional debasement of some currencies for political reasons make the analysis of markets in a variety of currencies a worthwhile approach to finding the "real" price level. This is similar to the adjustment of prices for inflation shown in Figure 4-4.

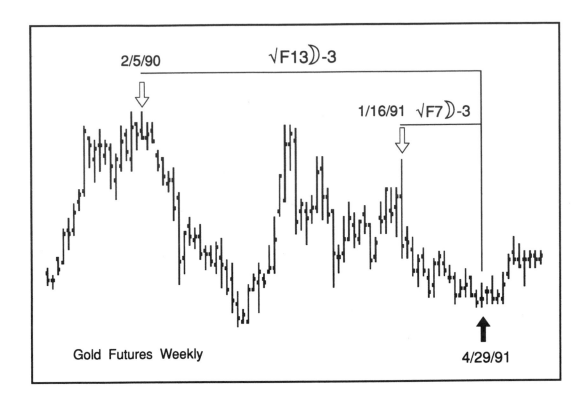

Gold		$\sqrt{f7}$	$\sqrt{f8}$	$\sqrt{f9}$	$\sqrt{f10}$	$\sqrt{f11}$	$\sqrt{f12}$	$\sqrt{f13}$
2/5/90		5/22/90	6/20/90	7/27/90	9/12/90	11/11/90	1/25/91	5/2/91
1/16/91		5/2/91	5/31/91	7/7/91	8/23/91	10/22/91	1/5/92	4/11/92

EXAMPLE 13

This and the next two examples are projected dates that lie on the same sequence, but are further apart in sequence numbers than golden sections. These examples nevertheless form reliable turns, but the expected type of turn (top or bottom) cannot be gauged until the time window arrives. The first example is from the gold futures market in 1991. The two tops on the odd additive sequence differ by six in sequence numbers. This means the ratio of the larger to the smaller distance is 4.235 or ϕ^3. The low occurred on the first day of the time window, three days before the projected dates.

100

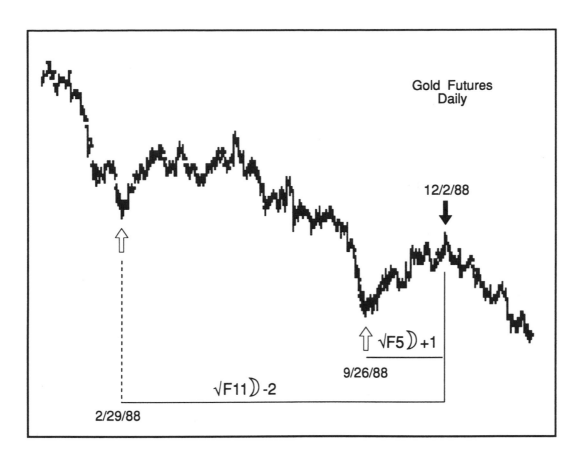

Gold		$\sqrt{f5}$	$\sqrt{f6}$	$\sqrt{f7}$	$\sqrt{f8}$	$\sqrt{f9}$	$\sqrt{f10}$	$\sqrt{f11}$
2/29/88		5/5/88	5/23/88	6/14/88	7/13/88	8/19/88	10/5/88	12/4/88
9/26/88		12/1/88	12/19/88	1/10/89	2/8/89	3/17/89	5/3/89	7/2/89

EXAMPLE 14

Gold futures in 1988 formed a time window in early December that was five calendar and three trading days wide. The top of December 2, 1988 fell in the center of the time window, the second trading day. The projected dates are both generated from the odd sequence, from turns that had produced multi-month moves. The top of December 2 led to a downturn of similar magnitude.

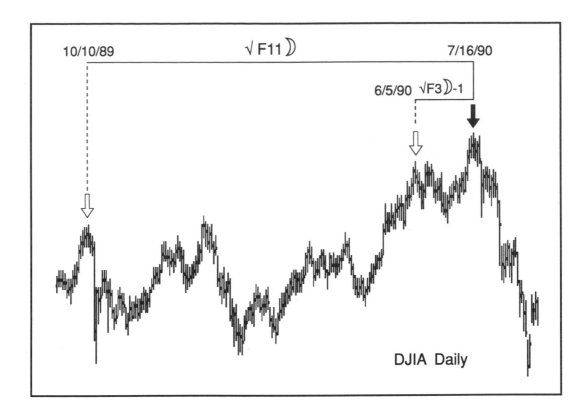

Dow		√f3		√f11
10/10/89		11/21/89		7/16/90
6/5/90		7/17/90		3/11/91

EXAMPLE 15

The 1990 price high in the DJIA occurred in a time window formed from the 1989 high of October 10 and the 1990 advance/decline line high of June 5. The projected dates were July 16 and 17. The closing high was made on July 16. The half hourly high was made on the 16th and equaled on the 17th. Subsequently, the market began a steep slide. The difference in sequence numbers here is eight. This is the maximum differential to use for clusters on the same sequence.

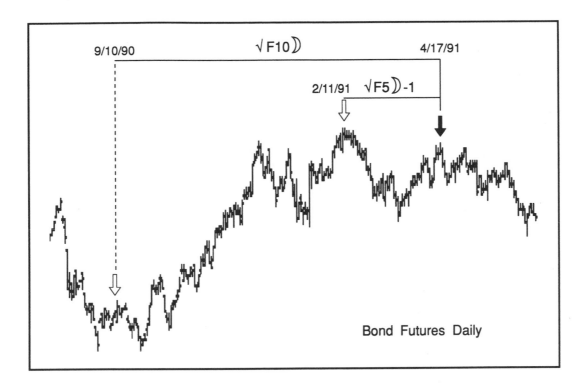

Bonds	√ƒ5	√ƒ6	√ƒ7	√ƒ8	√ƒ9	√ƒ10
9/10/90	11/15/90	12/3/90	12/25/90	1/23/91	3/1/91	4/17/91
2/11/91	4/18/91	5/6/91	5/28/91	6/26/91	8/2/91	9/18/91

EXAMPLE 16

The next set of examples involves projections from different (odd and even) additive sequences. In these cases, the projected dates must differ by no more than three days to be considered a cluster, rather than six days for dates on the same sequence. In this bond example from 1991, the projected dates differ by one day. The turn occurred on the first projected date, April 17. Both previous turns in this example were tops and the resulting turn is a top. However, there can be no reliable expectation of the type of resulting turn when the previous turns lie on different additive sequences. The sequence differential of five is the largest I use for clusters on different sequences.

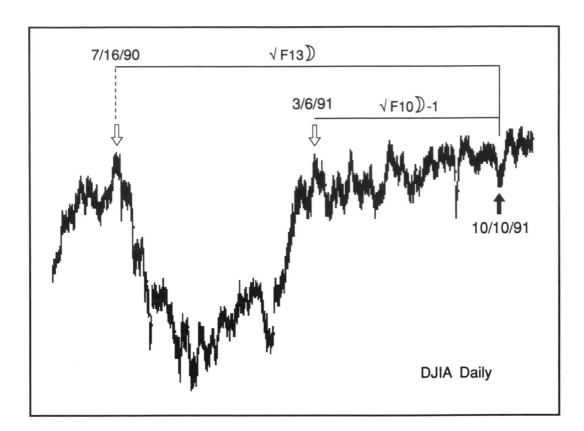

Dow		√*f*10	√*f*11	√*f*12	√*f*13
7/16/90		2/20/91	4/21/91	7/6/91	10/10/91
3/6/91		10/11/91	12/10/91	2/24/92	5/30/92

EXAMPLE 17

This Dow example is of a cluster in which the sequence numbers differ by three. The market turned on the first projected date. This low occurred near another cluster from a spiral of lows, shown in Figure 4-9. The cluster from the spiral projected a low for October 15. When two clusters are in proximity, the turn can occur at either one. The presence of this earlier cluster caused the arrival of the spiral low to be five days early. The magnitude of the low does not seem large on the chart. However, this low saw the highest thirty day Arms Index readings for 1991, indicating considerable selling at that time.

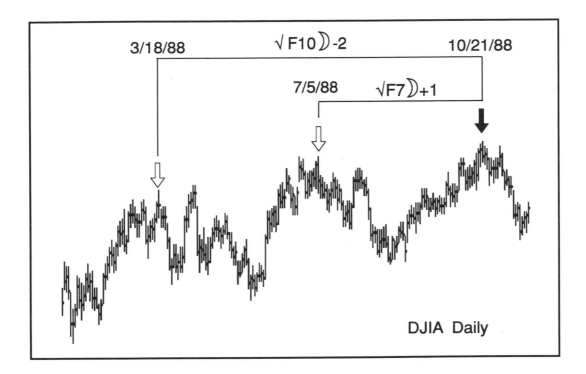

Dow	√f7	√f8	√f9	√f10
3/18/88	7/2/88	7/31/88	9/6/88	10/23/88
7/5/88	10/20/88	11/17/88	12/24/88	2/9/89

EXAMPLE 18

There is a three day difference in the projected dates in this example from the 1988 Dow. This is the maximum allowed for dates on different additive sequences. The time window stretches from three days before the second date to three days after the first. Therefore, the projected dates also define the time window. The top occurred on the second day in the time window.

EXAMPLE 19

The chart of gold from 1978 through early 1980 illustrates the effectiveness of the Spiral Calendar in emotional and dramatic markets.

The chart shows the eight largest magnitude turns leading to the final high of January 21, 1980. The final five turns on the chart all measure to two or more previous turns within the guidelines outlined in this chapter. Each of the final five turns could have been forecast with the Spiral Calendar to provide an extraordinary road map to one of the most remarkable trading markets of this century.

The second to last turn, November 20, 1979, is the apex of a triangular consolidation. It is detailed in Figure 6-3. The final high in gold occurred two trading days and four calendar days following a new moon.

Gold	√f4	√f6	√f8	√f9	√f10	√f11	√f12	√f13	√f14
3/8/78	4/28/78	5/31/78	7/21/78	8/27/78	10/13/78	12/12/76	2/25/79	6/2/79	10/2/79
4/25/78	6/15/78	7/18/78	9/7/78	10/14/78	11/30/78	1/29/79	4/14/79	7/20/79	11/19/79
10/30/78	12/20/78	1/22/79	3/14/79	4/20/79	6/6/79	8/5/79	10/19/79	1/24/80	5/25/80
11/30/78	1/20/79	2/22/79	4/14/79	5/21/79	7/7/79	9/5/79	11/19/79	2/24/80	6/25/80
2/22/79	4/14/79	5/17/79	7/7/79	8/13/79	9/29/79	11/28/79	2/11/80	5/18/80	9/17/80
4/16/79	6/6/79	7/9/79	8/29/79	10/5/79	11/21/79	1/20/80	4/4/80	7/10/80	11/9/80
10/2/79	11/22/79	12/25/79	2/14/80	3/22/80	5/8/80	7/7/80	9/20/80	12/26/80	4/27/81
11/20/79	1/10/80	2/12/80	4/3/80	5/10/80	6/26/80	8/25/80	11/8/80	2/13/81	6/15/81

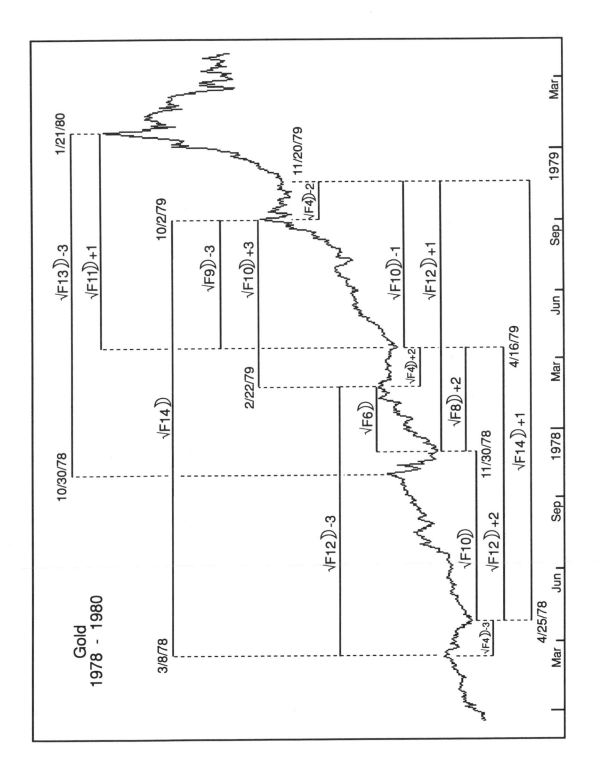

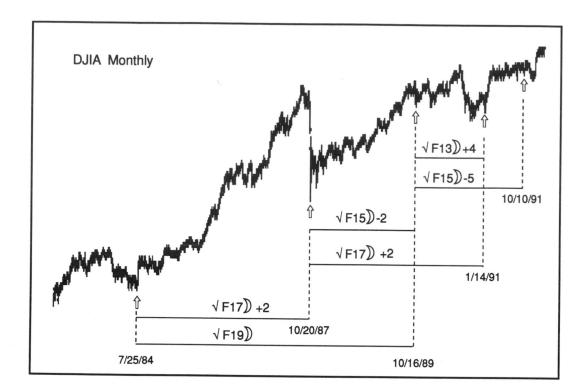

DJIA Monthly

√ F13$))$ +4

√ F15$))$ -5

10/10/91

√ F15$))$ -2

√ F17$))$ +2

1/14/91

√ F17$))$ +2

√ F19$))$

10/20/87

7/25/84

10/16/89

EXAMPLE 20; FINDING SPIRALS

The final example shows how to find spirals. Some spirals illustrated in Chapter 4 are depicted as structures measuring backwards from a date in the future, the focus. The same spiral depicted in Figure 4-8 is printed here, showing each turn's relationship to the other turns, rather than to the focus. The spreadsheet on page 110 shows how each turn moving forward on the odd sequence produces the next two turns on the spiral, followed by the focus, January 8, 1993. The October 1989 mini-crash and the January 1991 low are both golden sections from the two previous turns on the spiral. Knowledge of the focus, while helpful, is not necessary to forecast turns precisely. The focus is an idealized point in the future. For forecasting purposes, using the real turns from in the past, instead of the idealized future focus, is preferred for calculation. Calculating backwards from known foci or large clusters can be done, as will be shown in the next chapter.

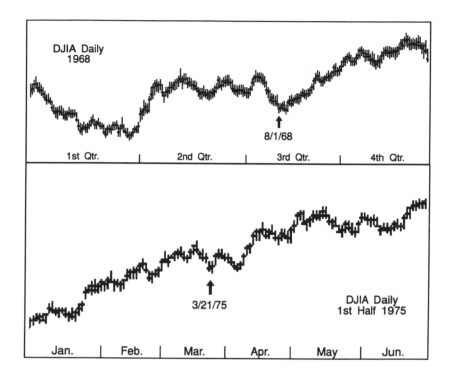

Dow		$\sqrt{f}22$	$\sqrt{f}23$	$\sqrt{f}24$	$\sqrt{f}25$	$\sqrt{f}26$	$\sqrt{f}27$	$\sqrt{f}28$
5/28/40		3/2/51	2/3/54	10/25/57	7/21/62	7/29/68	3/28/76	12/26/85
10/22/57		7/26/68	6/30/71	3/21/75	12/15/79	12/23/85	8/22/93	5/22/03

When does a spiral stop working? The most important facet to watch is the magnitude of the turns, followed by the precision. The relationship in Figure 5-7 in chapter five presents an example. A spiral was apparently in progress from the large magnitude lows of May 1940 and October 1957. Figure 5-7 shows the focus as December 27, 1985. The spreadsheet here shows the next two turns expected from the spiral and its focus. The charts above of 1968 and the first half of 1975 depict the sharply diminished magnitude of the turns when they occurred. The expected low of 1968 materialized, but *the magnitude of the decline was short and shallow. It was insignificant compared to the previous lows on the spiral.* This is the evidence that the spiral is diminishing. The spiral almost totally faded in 1975, as that decline was very short term. Note, though, that the precision of the 1975 low was exact to the day when measured from the 1957 low.

I want to stress the difference of the approach of this chapter to the previous two that revealed the structure of the Spiral Calendar. Chapters 4 and 5 admire the beauty of the market. Chapters 6 and 7 conquer it for the trader. Please appreciate the distinction.

The repeated and large scale examples of spirals at work demonstrate the structure of the market. This is not always helpful to traders. The spiral that occasionally misses or is imprecise can lose its usefulness as a tool. This chapter formulates parameters for finding realistic trading opportunities where the Spiral Calendar's precision and magnitude can provide an advantage. The approach outlined for trading is not meant to imply that structures that lie outside trading parameters do not belong to the Spiral Calendar. The parameters are just an attempt to add discipline, which is ultimately required in every trading endeavor.

Dow	√f11	√f12	√f13	√f14	√f15	√f16	√f17	√f18	√f19	√f20	√f21
7/25/84	4/30/85	7/14/85	10/19/85	2/19/86	7/24/86	2/8/87	10/18/87	9/3/88	10/16/89	3/20/91	1/8/93
10/20/87	7/25/88	10/9/88	1/13/89	5/16/89	10/18/89	5/5/90	1/12/91	11/29/91	1/10/93	6/14/94	4/5/96
10/16/89	7/22/90	10/5/90	1/10/91	5/13/91	10/15/91	5/1/92	1/8/93	11/25/93	1/7/95	6/10/96	4/1/98
1/14/91	10/20/91	1/4/92	4/9/92	8/10/92	1/12/93	7/30/93	4/8/94	2/23/95	4/7/96	9/8/97	7/1/99

CHAPTER 7

NIKKEI: A FORECASTING TUTORIAL

The Japanese stock market as measured by the Nikkei average has presented some of the most dramatic and potentially profitable price moves in recent years. The inflation of real estate and stock prices in the 1980s took the form of a classic speculative bubble. The emotion and lunacy of this market make it an ideal candidate for Spiral Calendar analysis.

There are myths about Japanese culture and business acumen that affect both Western and Japanese perceptions of the economic events in Japan. During the bull market, the perceived superiority of Japanese industry and finance supposedly justified the lunatic valuations placed on their assets. When the market began to decline, the alleged manipulative ability of the government fostered the belief that the decline could be arrested and that Japan would not suffer the tremendous economic crunch common to previous bursting bubbles. Instead, market forces have behaved as they always do, moving to one extreme and then reversing. Every indication as this market collapses (summer 1992) is that the other extreme, undervaluation, will be reached before recovery can begin.

Japanese culture has a characteristic that does impact its markets and affect Spiral Calendar analysis. The Japanese discourage individuality. To act in concert with the group is the expected form of behavior. In contrast, profitable trading requires a person to buy near market bottoms and to sell near tops. Bottoms occur when most people are selling, and tops occur when most people are buying. Successful trading requires a person to go against the behavior of the majority. This directly contradicts the accepted norm of Japanese social behavior. The emotional extremes and Spiral Calendar relationships of the Japanese market are better delineated than other markets because of this uniformity of group behavior.

This chapter covers a two year period in the Nikkei index beginning with its all time high of late 1989. The presentation of the analysis is slightly different from that in Chapter 6. The charts include the actual projected dates from the spreadsheet, rather than printing the spreadsheet itself. Each chart shows the market's movement up to the point of the illustrated cluster. In this way, all the Spiral Calendar information appears as it would at the time of the forecasting decisions. The daily data available for this analysis begins in September 1986, restricting the ability to forecast large magnitude turns.

The analysis begins at the end of 1989, with the Nikkei at its all time high. Figure 7-1 shows the large cluster of Spiral Calendar relationships pointing to the final days of 1989. The bottom chart shows weekly prices for three years, and the top chart daily prices for the final seven months of 1989. Three lows in the market all lie on the odd Spiral Calendar sequence, projecting December 26, 1989 for a turn. One market top lies on the even sequence and also projects December 26. Another top on the even sequence projects December 30. Two additional lows, also on the odd sequence, project to the same time vicinity, plus or minus ten days from the cluster, implying an associative relationship. Taken together, the lows form a perfect spiral of five lows on the odd sequence, with a focus a few days after the winter solstice. A check of the ephemeris shows there is no full moon at this time, rather the new moon is December 28.

The structure is similar to the perfect spirals of lows shown in Chapter 4, except that the focus is a new moon rather than a full moon. A sharply rising market into a large cluster at a new moon indicates a potential top on the new moon. The magnitude of the largest relationship, $\sqrt{F}16$, indicates this will be an important top. The time window formed by the cluster runs from Wednesday, December 27 through Friday the 29th.

The all time high in Japanese stock prices occurred on December 29. Traders following the aggressive approach outlined in Chapter 6 would have begun selling on the 28th, one day before the high and the day of the new moon. Traders following the conservative approach would have sold on January 4, the first day of trading after the top when prices broke decisively down, confirming the importance of the time window. Both approaches afforded excellent trading entry points for a short sale or exit points for longs who rode the bull market up.

Once the trade is in place, the $\sqrt{F}n$ magnitude should help determine the size of the expected move. Too often, traders expect that a multi-month move is underway, but they exit their position after only weeks or days. This forecast, because of the large sequence numbers involved, implies a move down of significant duration.

The advantage that precision allows in formulating risk/reward strategies is worth repeating here. If you sell the day before or after a very important turn *and* you know that turn is very important *and* you know that the price level of the turn will not be significantly broken if you are correct, *then* you have a very small risk between the entry price and the stop point where you will take losses. Combine that with the large size of the expected move, and the risk/reward equation is very favorable.

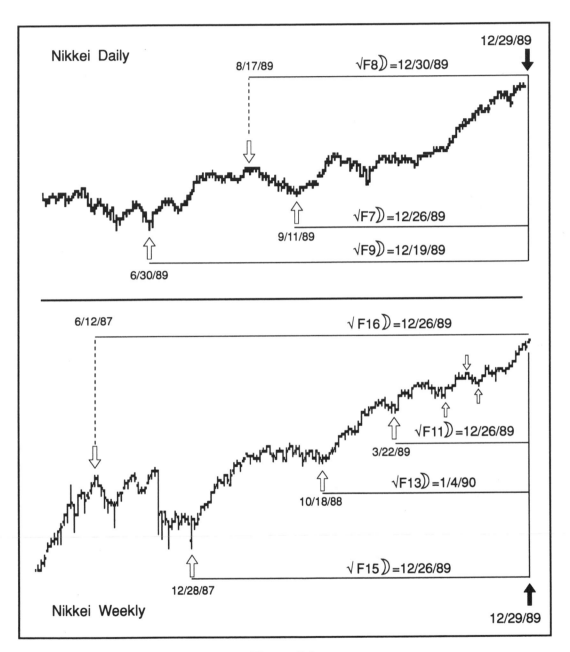

Figure 7-1

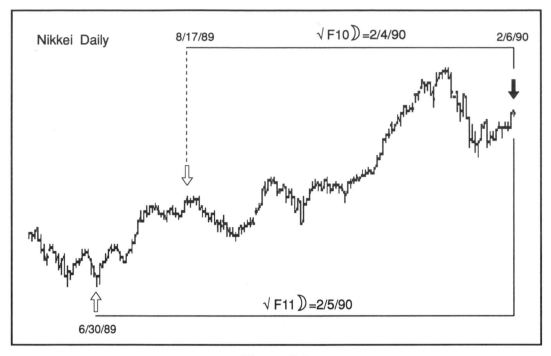

Figure 7-2

Figure 7-2 depicts the Nikkei average five weeks after the top. The market is rising into a time window of Friday, February 2 through Wednesday, February 7. The market topped on Tuesday, February 6, within two calendar days of both projected dates. The sizes of the Spiral Calendar relationships are smaller than those of the December 29 top, and the resulting magnitude confirms that this is a lesser magnitude turn. Good trading manuals stress the importance of being aware of the larger trend and not trading against it. Date clusters imply trend changes, thus the market action into the date cluster provides clues to the larger trend. Rising markets into date clusters during bear markets imply the resumption of the larger bear trend, while in bull markets they may be the termination of the trend. The converse is true for bottoms. We assume, because of magnitude, that the December 29 Nikkei top marked the beginning of a large decline. The sign we watch for to indicate the end of the major decline is for the market to trade down into a time window of magnitude and then reverse. This is exactly what happens in the next example.

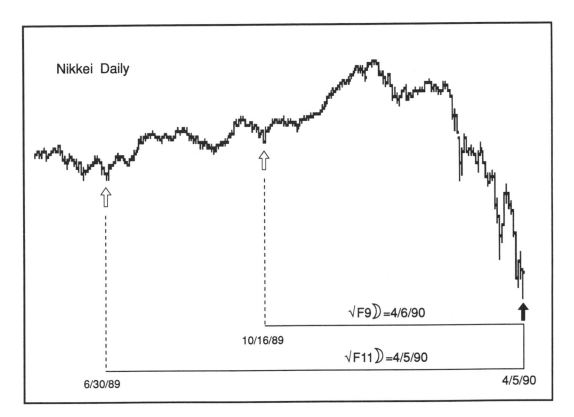

Figure 7-3

Now we come to the first week of April 1990. The daily chart of the Nikkei index, Figure 7-3, shows a price breakdown from the tops of December and early February. Two short term spike lows had formed in February and March, but there were no time windows on those dates. The market confirmed they were not important bottoms by trading through to lower prices before significant rallies could develop. A golden section ($\sqrt{F9}$ and $\sqrt{F11}$) is indicated by projected dates on April 5 and 6. The previous turns are lows, signaling a potential bottom here. The selloff into April 5 displays extreme emotion. For traders short from the December top, this is definitely a time to take profits . Aggressive traders can buy for a rally. The market obliged with a sustained rally from the low made precisely on one of the two projected dates. The next example shows the extent of the rally.

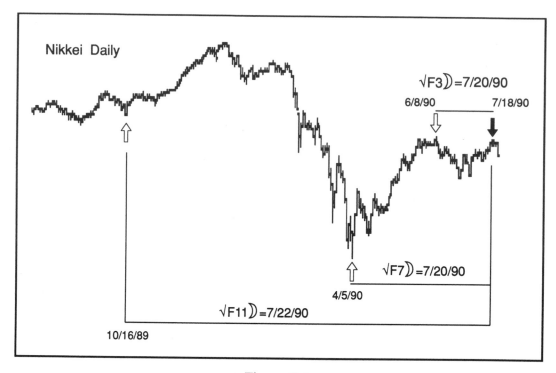

Figure 7-4

Figure 7-4 shows the Nikkei's position in late July of 1990. The rally from the April low was substantial, stopping on June 8, when there was *no time window*. After heading down again in June, prices rallied once more to near, but just shy of, the June 8 top. The chart shows three projected dates, a large cluster, on the odd sequence forming a time window from July 19 through 23. Here the market topped the day before the time window, the 18th. It is, however, within two days of two projected dates, meeting the criteria for precision if the third date is not considered part of the cluster. In large cluster situations, there are multiple ways to calculate the time window depending on which projected dates are used. The market action is the key to finding the exact turn. The Spiral Calendar cluster alerts the trader to the possible trend change somewhere in this vicinity. The move down on the 20th confirms the expectation. Even though the downturn was underway, the bulk of the price move was still ahead. Without the help of the Spiral Calendar forecast, the drop on July 20 may seem to be just a pause in the larger uptrend.

It is always a good idea to look for large magnitude Spiral Calendar relationships that will define the major trends. Even if they are far in the future, they can lend perspective to market expectations.

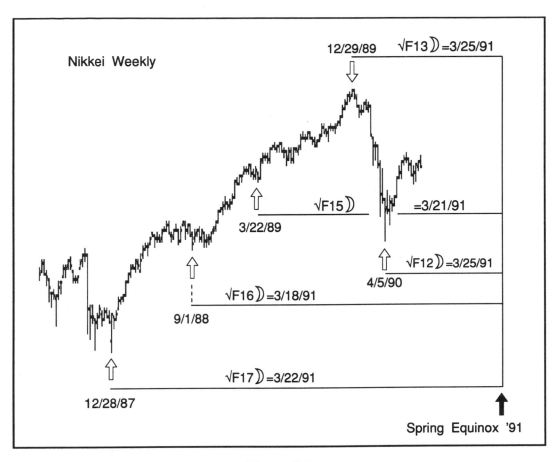

Figure 7-5

The weekly chart in Figure 7-5 shows five projected dates in the vicinity of the 1991 spring equinox. Three of the previous turns are arguably the most important on the chart, the December 1987 low, the December 1989 high and the April 1990 low. The ephemeris shows no new moon near the spring equinox in 1991. This is not a new moon, spring equinox spiral. This large cluster of dates is the most important time frame on the horizon for the next twelve months in the Nikkei average. *If this point marks a low, it might well be the end to the bear market that began in December 1989. If it is a market high, it could present a selling opportunity equal to that of December 1989.*

With five points contributing to this cluster, it is possible that future turns between here and March 1991 will also project to this point. A calculation backward from the average of these projected dates will provide additional places to look for turns, particularly if they are confirmed by conventional clusters. The spreadsheet that follows shows the dates back from March 23, 1991.

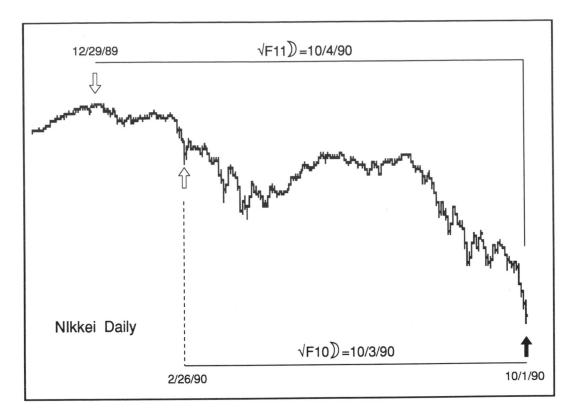

Figure 7-6

Backwards	$\sqrt{f2}$	$\sqrt{f3}$	$\sqrt{f4}$	$\sqrt{f5}$	$\sqrt{f6}$	$\sqrt{f7}$	$\sqrt{f8}$	$\sqrt{f9}$
3/23/91	2/21/91	2/9/91	1/31/91	1/16/91	12/29/90	12/7/90	11/8/90	10/2/90

From the identified top in late July, the Nikkei traded down, convincingly penetrating the April 1990 low. Figure 7-6 brings us to October 1, where a time window occurs from Monday the 1st to Friday the 5th. The calculation backward from March 23, 1991 includes October 2 at $\sqrt{F9}$. A sharp rally on October 2 signaled that a bottom on the Nikkei average had occurred on October 1, within the forecasted time window.

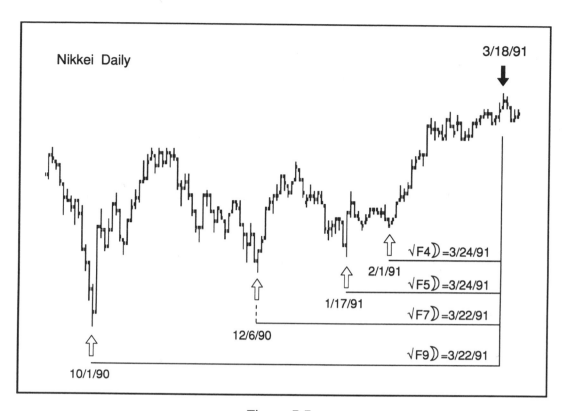

Figure 7-7

Figure 7-7 shows the market's movements after the October 1990 low. The backward calculation produced three more lows, all precise to within one day. The rising market of February and early March indicated that the large cluster near the spring equinox would be a high. The most important knowledge from the Spiral Calendar here is the *relative magnitude* of the upcoming spring 1991 high versus the October 1990 low. The large sequence numbers and important previous turns contributing to the spring high indicate that it is *more important than the October low*, indicating that the market will likely penetrate the October low on the downside before penetrating the spring 1991 high on the upside.

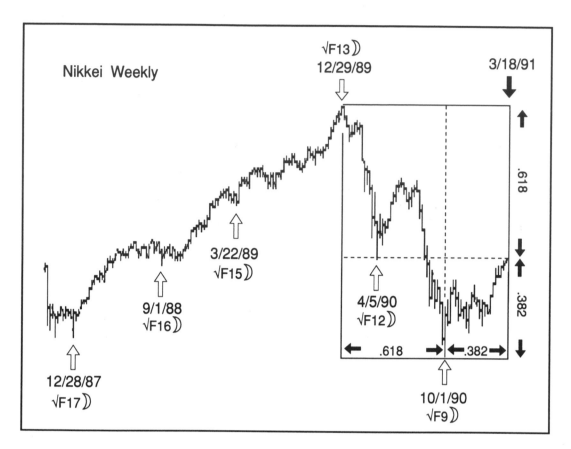

Figure 7-8

The top in March 1991 occurred on the 18th, the earliest date in the large cluster. Figure 7-8 illustrates the Fibonacci price relationships at that time. On March 18 exactly, the Nikkei average temporarily crossed the point marking a .382 price retracement of the December 1989 to October 1990 decline. The analysis of price targets is not the subject of this book. However, the high, the low and the retracement high are in golden sections to each other in both *price and time*. The magnitude of the date cluster, combined with the precision in the price dimension, produced an extremely accurate forecast.

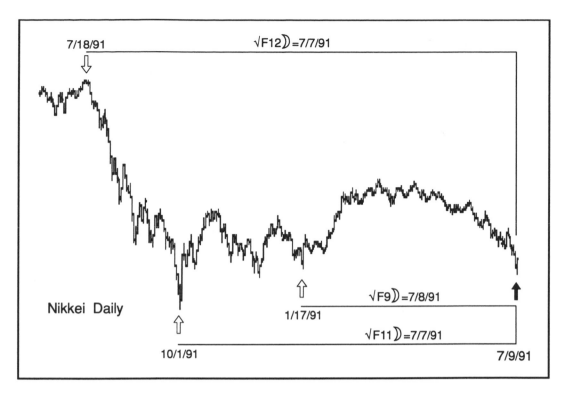

Figure 7-9

The Nikkei average did not drop dramatically after the March 1991 high. Prices moved sideways for weeks without showing deterioration. Markets have a way of shaking those without patience from their positions. The Spiral Calendar, by giving us a defined time window for a turn, allows us the freedom to let the market unfold as slowly or quickly as it likes. *As long as our price high in the cluster is not significantly exceeded, there is no reason to suspect that the forecast is wrong.* This allows for a patient and rewarding approach to trading. Less second guessing means less stressful trading. The Nikkei rewarded patient bears with an accelerated downturn in June. The market began to exhibit emotion in early July. A time window from Friday, July 5 to Wednesday, July 10 is indicated by the cluster in Figure 7-9. The market traded lower into Tuesday morning the 9th before reversing.

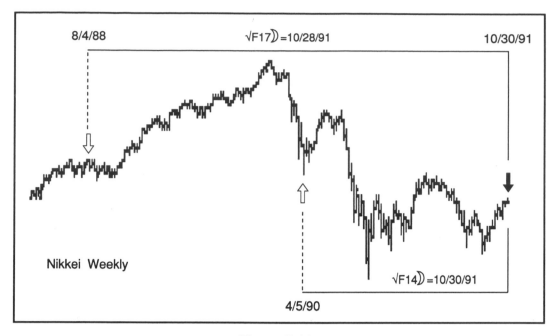

Figure 7-10

The low of July 9 marked only a temporary bottom. Prices soon fell back to make a lower low on August 20, when there was no time window. A larger rally then began, carrying the market up into late October. Two date clusters existed in late October. One was a large cluster of four dates between October 23 and 25, the other a cluster of two dates on October 28 and 30. The second cluster, shown in Figure 7-10, contained larger relationships, in terms of sequence number, than the first. Prices continued higher through the first cluster into the date projected from the April 1990 low. The two years of Nikkei history presented three excellent selling opportunities so far. This was the fourth.

The final chart, Figure 7-11, shows the Nikkei average to the date of this writing. White arrows on the chart mark the trading opportunities presented in this chapter. Our approach has been to locate the important market turning points rather than every swing in prices. The fact that the Spiral Calendar could consistently forecast the major turns makes it a valuable method.

The chart also shows the overriding structure that has governed the Nikkei in this time period, a new moon, spring equinox spiral with a focus in 1993. This is a beautiful pattern in time. I have presented the governing focus at the end of the chapter to stress that the understanding of larger spirals and foci are not required for consistent Spiral Calendar forecasting.

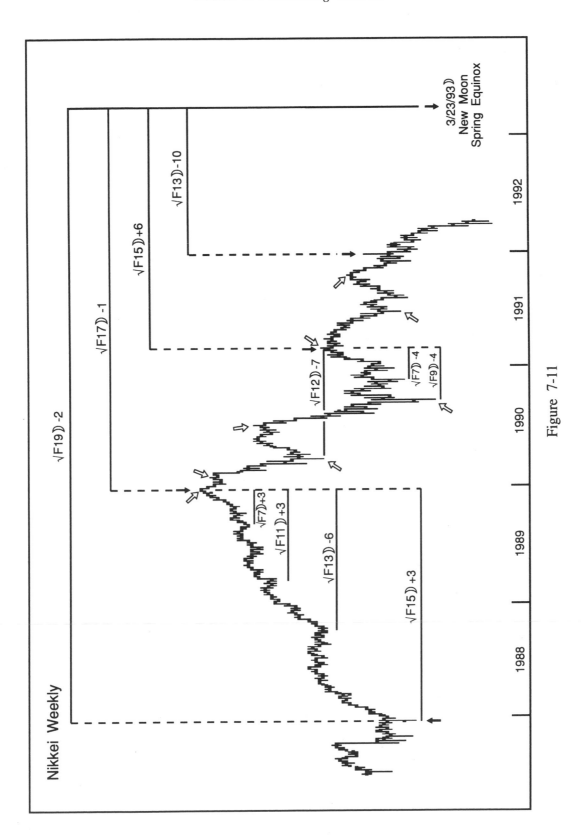

Figure 7-11

PART III

PAST FUTURE & BEYOND

CHAPTER 8

SPIRAL CALENDAR PAST

THE SPIRAL CALENDAR IN THE ANCIENT WORLD?

The Spiral Calendar has two components, the lunar and the spiral or Fibonacci. Chapter 3 explored the presence of the golden mean and Fibonacci ratios in the ancient world. The phi ratio and proportion was sacred to ancient cultures, particularly Egypt and Greece, and possibly Babylon. Now it is time to look at the lunar aspect of the Spiral Calendar for a connection with the ancient lunar calendar and its associated holy days. The reason for my curiosity in this regard is that in every year in the 20th century with a nasty October market slide, the selloff began after a market peak was made on or near the Jewish holy day of Yom Kippur. What was the meaning of Yom Kippur and what were its origins?

YOM KIPPUR

Yom Kippur falls on the 10th day of Tishri, the 7th lunar month on the Jewish Calendar. The first day of Tishri, the new moon, marks the Jewish New Year. These two holy days are considered the most solemn in the Jewish calendar and are known as the "High Holy Days." Yom Kippur is the "day of atonement," when Jews are to atone with fasting for their past mistakes before God. The ancient myth associated with Yom Kippur is that a person's behavior during the period between Rosh Hashanah and Yom Kippur will form the basis of a judgment by God which will determine his fate for the coming year. The judgment is written in three books, one for the good, one for the doubtful and one for the damned. Where does this myth come from? In 1987 and 1929, anyone who shorted stocks during those ten days was judged as successful by the market in the following weeks and, likewise, anyone who bought stocks during those ten days were quickly judged as "damned."

CALENDARS AND HOLIDAYS

Stephen Langdon was professor of Assyriology at Oxford in the 1930s. He delivered a series of lectures at the British Academy in 1933 entitled *Babylonian Menologies and the Semitic Calendars*. A menology is a calendar of months from the Greek *meno*, moon. One point of the lectures was to demonstrate the connections from ancient calendars' holidays and holy days to our present ones in both timing and symbolism. Jewish and Christian holidays can be traced to Babylon, and the Babylonian holidays can be traced to ancient Sumeria. The holidays we inherit contain the same timing and symbolism, but usually not the meaning of the ancient originals. Langdon describes how a minority culture will absorb the traditions of a dominating culture, although they will ascribe their own meanings to those traditions.

The Christian Christmas and the Jewish Hanukkah are an example of this "borrowing" phenomenon. Both holidays have their root in the Babylonian celebration of the winter solstice. The meaning of the original Babylonian solstice holiday was twofold: to celebrate the rebirth of the sun, which at the solstice stopped its descent in the sky and began its ascent back to the zenith in the summer; and to celebrate, as Langdon calls it, "the genius of the hearth." This was man's mastery of fire that enabled him to overcome the dark and cold of winter. They celebrated this mastery at the darkest time of the year, the winter solstice, by lighting torches and braziers. The meaning of the original Babylonian holiday, fire and solstice, do not survive, but the symbols, light and birth, are the hallmarks of our current celebrations.

The Jewish festival Hanukkah is known as the "festival of lights." The meaning, the relighting of the temple lights after being extinguished, is different, but the symbolism of light is the same. The timing of the Jewish and Christian holidays are the same, except applied to different calendars. Hanukkah falls on the 25th of the lunar month, and Christmas is the 25th of December on the solar calendar.

Why are holidays inherited from culture to culture? Think of the situation for the early Christians. They wished to convert people to their beliefs, but people naturally didn't want to forsake their traditions and holidays. The Christians adapted their new meanings to the old symbols and timing. The process is happening again today. Some African-Americans do not feel that Christmas and Hanukkah are their holidays. To celebrate their own culture, they have begun a holiday called Kwanzaa, celebrated in late December. The meaning of the holiday is their own, but among the symbols they use is the lighting of candles, just like the candles on the Menorah of the Jews, the Christmas lights of the Christians and the torches of the Babylonians five thousand years ago.

Easter and Passover have their roots in the most important holiday of the Babylonians, their New Year. The Babylonian New Year was the new moon nearest the spring equinox. Note that it was not the equinox itself that was the holiday, but the combination of the two calendars, the solar equinox and the new moon which created the holiday, and the key date was provided by the moon. Our Easter and Passover are still set with the lunar calendar. Easter is the first Sunday after the first full moon after the spring equinox. Passover is 14 days after the new moon near the spring equinox. The symbolism of Easter has its roots in the Babylonian calendar. The death, then resurrection of Christ after three days, describes exactly the course of the new moon. It dies, and three days later is resurrected. The Babylonians, who believed that the position of the sun and moon determined men's fate, worshipped one particular new moon over all others, the spring equinox new moon. I have discovered the importance of that particular new moon in its tendency to be the focus of important Spiral Calendar sequences. See Figures 4-11, 4-12, 4-13 and 4-14.

The Jewish Yom Kippur derives from a holy day in Babylon that was celebrated on the 9th day of Teshrit, the 7th month. The Babylonians also celebrated a second New Year in the fall that is comparable to the Jewish Rosh Hashanah. The symbolism of the atonement and fasting of Yom Kippur is also part of the Babylonian holiday. More interesting is that the myth of the judgment and the book of fates is from Babylon as well. The judgment of the Jewish Yom Kippur is the same as the judgment of the scales of Libra, which is in the Babylonian zodiac and falls at the same time of year. The Jews acquired these traditions during and following the Babylonian captivity in the 5th century B.C., when Jews were exiled to Babylon. Prior to this time, the Jews did have a holiday at the time of Yom Kippur, but it was primarily a temple purification rite which involved the priests of the temple, not the public at large. Their concept of atonement can be dated as being not earlier than the captivity.[1] Why did the Jews adopt the *meaning* of the Babylonian holiday, and not just the timing and symbols? Let's take a look at some history of the Mesopotamians and the time period when the Jews were under Babylonian influence.

THE MESOPOTAMIANS

The Mesopotamians lived in the valleys formed by the Tigris and Euphrates rivers. They included the Sumerians, Babylonians and Assyrians. The Sumerians came first and are thought to be the world's oldest civilization. They were the first to live in cities and the first to use writing. It is not known where they originally came from. Their language was Sumerian. The Babylonians and Assyrians followed the Sumerians. They both spoke Akkadian and, unlike the Sumerians, were a Semitic people. They lived side by side, the Assyrians in the North and the Babylonians in the South, sometimes at peace and sometimes at war. These Mesopotamians preserved the Sumerian language, though they did not speak it. They took from the Sumerians their culture, calendar, holidays and many of their gods.

---

[1] *Encyclopaedia Judaica.* 5. 1387.

There are two characteristics of the Babylonians and Assyrians that I will describe. These characteristics were unique to their culture, and ultimately provide for an interesting speculation about the Spiral Calendar in the ancient world.

The Babylonians and Assyrians used the tradition of writing, inherited from the earlier Sumerians, in order to keep thousands of years of detailed records of events in their world along with the physical and astronomic conditions present at the time of these events. Thousands of these records survive as *omen texts*. Oppenheim states that this methodical approach moved divination "from the realm of folklore to the level of scientific activity," and that the result was "high scholarly achievement."[2] This tradition of observation and record keeping was the origin of the Mesopotamian belief that the position of the sun and moon affected the actions and fate of men, what has come down to us as astrology. The modern concept of astrology is different from what was practiced by the Babylonians and Assyrians of 2200 BC to 650 BC. The original concept was not that the position of planets at the time of your birth would determine your life, only that the position of the sun and moon *now* would affect your actions and fate *now*. The addition of time of birth, the *horoscope*, into astrology did not come until later, about 400 BC after the age of methodical and consistent record keeping.[3] The advent of this bastardization of a valid concept was consistent with the abandonment of scientific observation within the culture.

We know that the Babylonians and Assyrians recorded the position of the sun and moon at the time of extraordinary events. If, over the course of thousands of years, they experienced financial manias and panics, their record keeping would have noticed similarities in the position of the sun and moon when these panics occurred. Look at it from our perspective. Suppose we were using a lunar calendar instead of a solar one in the 20th century. In 1987, when the market crash fell on the exact anniversary of the 1929 crash, the reaction among people and scientists would have been dramatic. Yet, since we don't keep records of the sun's and moon's position at the time of extraordinary financial events, the lunar significance of the crash almost went unnoticed. *Almost.*

Did the Mesopotamians have financial manias and panics? Economic manias and panics are not part of the history of other past western cultures, such as the Greeks and Romans. What do we know about economic life in Babylon and Assyria? *The Mesopotamians were distinguished by their economic success.* The wealth and riches of Babylon and Ninevah were legendary. *Uniquely among cultures, their economic system allowed for capital to be traded as a commodity and for interest to be charged for its use, usury.* The trading of capital allows for economic growth and speculation. Oppenheim reports that the omen texts reveal

> "a remarkable degree of economic mobility: the poor expect to
> become rich and the rich are afraid of becoming poor."[4]

---

[2]*Oppenheim.* page 210.
[3]*Ibid.* page 224.
[4]*Ibid.* page 87.

Economic mobility is a hallmark of our modern Western free markets. Free markets, including one for the lending of money, allow the poor to convert good ideas to wealth and allow the rich to lose their fortunes through bad loans and investments. Ancient Babylon and Assyria share with our modern times the operation of free capital markets, which can result in excessive speculation and panic. It is also interesting that we learn of the Mesopotamians' economic mobility through the omen texts. This inclusion indicates that they looked to the position of the sun and moon for information on their financial fate.

The Mesopotamians could indeed have experienced financial panics and manias. Once experienced, they had the knowledge, gained by systematic record keeping, to discover the lunar piece of the Spiral Calendar puzzle. Left unanswered is the question, is Yom Kippur's myth and meaning, judgment and atonement, a remnant of the ancient experience with October panics? Why did the Jews adopt *all* the aspects of the Babylonian holiday, its myth, symbols *and meaning*? The answers, I believe, are related.

THE BIBLICAL CONNECTION

The 7th century BC was the apex of the Assyrian empire. This empire was the greatest yet known to man. Assyrians ruled from Egypt to what is now Iran. The capital of the empire, Ninevah, reached its zenith from 705 BC to 680 BC.[5] The Hebrews prospered under Assyrian rule. They had to pay tribute to the Assyrian king, but in good times there was enough to go around. This was the time of Isaiah the prophet. As biblical scholars describe the period, "Isaiah's career began at a time of growing prosperity that brought comfort and luxury...The economic and political outlook never seemed brighter."[6] Isaiah prophesied doom for the people based on the greed and materialism that was overcoming them.

The Assyrians' final king, Assurbanipal (668-627 BC), ruled over the cultural peak of the empire. This is the time period of the "Dying Lioness" relief found at Ninevah, which contains φ proportions (see page 36). Assurbanipal's library at Ninevah was the largest in the near East and provides scholars with volumes of data from the period. Remarkably, however, no documentation exists from the final ten years of his rule. The empire collapsed after his death. Within twenty years, in 612 BC, Ninevah was obliterated from the face of the Earth. The rapidity of the collapse is consistent with what would result from the bursting of a speculative bubble with ensuing widespread poverty. This was the end of a prosperous and economically secure age.

The 6th century BC was a very different story. The near East was dominated by the Chaldean dynasty, which ruled from Babylon. They were not able to reestablish the far flung empire of the Assyrians. The Chaldeans were prosperous themselves, but their neighbors had a different fate. Many of the Hebrews were taken captive to Babylon, the

---

[5]*Encyclopaedia Judaica.* 12. 1170.
[6]*Ibid.* 9 47.

first in 605 BC, 7 years after the fall of Ninevah. The Chaldean king, Nebuchadnezzar, destroyed Jerusalem in 586 BC. The palace and temple were looted, the city walls dismantled and the city burned to the ground.

The Biblical prophet of this era was Ezekial. He was among the Jewish captives in Babylon. This is the time when the Hebrews adopted the Babylonian calendar. Biblical scholars place the adoption of the self denial aspects of Yom Kippur, the fasting and atonement,[7] and the myth of the judgment of fates in this period.[8] Another change in biblical attitude from this time was towards usury, the lending of money for interest. Before the captivity, it was frowned upon. *Encyclopaedia Judaica* makes the following distinction: "It was only in the prophesies of Ezekial that usury came to be identified with the gravest of crimes."[9] *The adoption in early October of a holy day that prescribed self denial and the prohibition of the charging of interest were both instituted after the greatest economic collapse the world had ever seen.*

The Mesopotamian version of the holy day that featured the myth of the judgment was much older than this time period. Langdon places it before 2000 BC. The origin of the holy day could not have been the observance of a lunar associated mania and panic at the peak of the Assyrian empire. However, it is possible that a holy day already in place could be observed to relate to the sequence of manias and panics in the speculative froth of the Assyrian empire at Ninevah. Remember the quote above from Oppenheim, "the poor *expect* to become rich." (italics mine) To *expect* financial gain to come your way is certainly a sentiment of a topping market or empire. The Hebrews may have observed that the people who practiced the rituals of self denial in October during the heyday of greed in Ninevah and Babylon had spared themselves from the ensuing panic. Then, with an understanding of the power of the prophesy forecast in the lunar calendar and the myth of the judgment, they adopted it as their own.

The Hebrew observation of the Assyrian rituals of self denial in October exist in the bible as the book of Jonah. Jonah is sent to Ninevah to prophesy the downfall of the city within forty days because of the Ninevite's wickedness. At first, he does not go and is swallowed by a fish. Then, he goes to Ninevah, described as a great city of three days journey from end to end. This description of the size of Ninevah places the story of Jonah at the time of Ninevah's peak. He tells his prophesy to the king, and the king orders a fast and the wearing of sackcloth as atonement. The city is spared. Jonah's prophesy does not come to pass *because* it is believed.

If Jonah's prophesy was the forecast of a market crash based on the lunar calendar and made at the time of the holy days of atonement, it would have preceded an expected market crash by forty days or less. A final observation is the fact that the Book of Jonah is read to this day in its entirety in the Jewish temple on Yom Kippur. This is the link between the current Jewish holy day of Yom Kippur, which is the date of market tops

---

[7]*Ibid.*
[8]*Langdon.* pp 100.
[9]*Encyclopaedia Judaica.* 16 28.

Mesopotamian New Year	New Moon Spring Equinox	Full Moon Spring Equinox	
	New Moon Summer Solstice	Full Moon Summer Solstice	
	New Moon Fall Equinox	Full Moon Fall Equinox	
	New Moon Winter Solstice	Full Moon Winter Solstice	Stonehenge Alignment

Table 8-1. The eight lunar phase/solar season combinations.

preceding crashes on the lunar calendar, and the origin of that holy day during a time of economic excess followed by collapse. The fasting and the wearing of the sackcloth described in Jonah survive to the present as the methods of atonement and self denial in the Jewish ritual.

The part of the story of Jonah in which he is swallowed by the fish can now be seen in a different light. The time inside the fish is described as a journey to the nether world for three days and three nights. There is a figure in mythology which journeyed to the nether world for three days and three nights, the moon in its new phase. In this sense, it was not a human who forecast the doom of Ninevah, but the moon itself.

The Biblical role of the concept of usury in economic history is important. White, in *Crashes and Panics*, details the role of the cost of money during panics. The speculators who have borrowed too much are caught in the vise as interest rates reach unbelievable levels. The fervent Biblical prohibition against usury, which originated at these times, had an effect on Western economies for two thousand years. The Catholic church inherited this attitude towards usury from the Jews, and enforced it even more strictly. The subject of usury was always linked to the greed and excess of Babylon. It was not until the reformation in the 16th century that the church's hold over economic policy was broken. Within one hundred years, modern times saw its first financial mania and panic, the tulip craze of 1636.

STONEHENGE

Table 8-1 shows the eight possible combinations of lunar phases and solar seasons. Of these eight, I have found only two that seem to have repeated importance as Spiral Calendar foci, the new moon at spring equinox and the full moon at winter solstice. The new moon near spring equinox was chosen among the eight to mark the beginning of the calendar and the most important holiday of the year for the Mesopotamians. The full moon at winter solstice was not of particular importance to the Mesopotamians, but it does figure in the calendar of another culture.

Alban Wall, in an article titled, *Stonehenge and the Calendar of Coligny*, argues convincingly that the Celts built Stonehenge. He also shows how Stonehenge is the most remarkable of calendars, as it is lunar-solar. Instead of keeping just lunar time, as most ancient calendars did, or solar time like modern calendars, Stonehenge accurately kept both forms of time. Lunar and solar time are in agreement nearly every nineteen years. That means that the moon will be in the same phase on the same solar day. This is the Metonic cycle, named after the Greek, Meton, though Stonehenge shows that this cycle was understood by the Celts significantly earlier.

The Celtic calendar's New Year falls near the winter solstice. Wall demonstrates how the most significant alignment at Stonehenge occurs at sunset in the years when the moon is full at the winter solstice. At this time, the sun sets between the great stone trilithon and the full moon rises over the solstice marker, an impressive sight.

The Celts, like the Mesopotamians, chose one of the eight combinations of lunar phases/solar seasons to denote time's ordering process over life in their religious calendar. It is remarkable that, among eight lunar-solar periods, the two that are of significance in the Spiral Calendar are *the same two* that these ancient cultures revered. We usually consider the calendar's role in religion as that of telling us when to worship. It may be that the ancients perceived the process behind the calendar itself as the object of worship.

There is no clay tablet proving the Mesopotamians knew of the Spiral Calendar. Yet, we know that they believed in a connection between the moon and economic behavior. The components of the Spiral Calendar were important to ancient cultures. It is fascinating that at least two ancient cultures, Egypt and Greece, chose to build their most important and enduring monuments with phi proportions. Additionally, at least two other ancient cultures, Mesopotamian and Jewish, chose their most important holy days at certain lunar phases near solar seasonal changes. These are threads that connect the knowledge and actions of the ancients and come down to our time as ritual and custom. In this so called age of science, we too readily dismiss much of our inherited culture. We do not have a reasoning power or brain capacity greater than that of those who lived three or five thousand years ago. In the case of the Mesopotamians, we have not begun to equal the tradition of observation of nature *over time* that they accomplished.

MORTUI VIVOS DOCENT.

CHAPTER 9

BEYOND MARKETS

The focus of this book is on patterns of emotional behavior in markets. Emotional behavior is not limited to markets, however; it is everywhere. If the Spiral Calendar is evidence of the basic ordering process for human life, then its patterns should exist in other forms of group emotional behavior. The difficulty in looking beyond markets for Spiral Calendar links is the lack of data. Financial markets lend themselves to precise analysis because of the availability of precise data. With non-market events, locating the key emotional turning point in time can be a more subjective exercise. I proceed with an awareness of those limitations. I have not undertaken a search for Spiral Calendar relationships beyond markets. However, in two separate events that captured headlines, I noticed time periods that were Spiral Calendar units. In each instance, I investigated further, with remarkable results.

THE COLLAPSE OF COMMUNISM

News accounts of the fall of the Berlin Wall mentioned that the Wall had stood for just over 28 years. I knew that 28.2 years was a Spiral Calendar time length, and was curious as to how precise the measurement was. The Wall was not built in a day, but its origin is considered to be the day East Germany sealed the border with West Berlin to stem a rising tide of border crossings in late July and early August 1961. The flood of East Germans into West Berlin in 1961 had reached hundreds of people per hour. It was certainly an emotional event. The Brandenburg Gate was sealed by East German troops on Sunday, August 12, 1961 early in the morning. This time is taken as the beginning of the Berlin Wall.

Spiral Calendar and the Collapse of Communism

Berlin Wall Sealed	√ F26 ☽ +27 days	Berlin Wall Falls
12 Aug. 1961	.618	9 Nov. 1989

German Surrender	√ F28 ☽ -3 days	First German Elections
7 May 1945	1.0	2 Dec. 1990

Russian Revolution	√ F30 ☽ +13 days	Bolsheviks Fall
8 Nov. 1917	1.618	22 Aug. 1991

Figure 9-1

The 26th Spiral Calendar time unit is 10,289 days, or 348.41 moons. Add this time length to August 12, 1961 and the result is October 13, 1989. October 1989 was the month of crucial events leading to the fall of the Wall. Freedom demonstrations broke out across East Germany. The event seen by the Germans as the turning point was the massive demonstration in Leipzig on October 9. Fifty thousand people attended this rally, the largest of the demonstrations. At this point, the East German government realized it had lost control. The people were no longer afraid of the army. They were demanding the right to do what the army had stopped in August of 1961, the ability to leave. On November 4, the East Germans opened the border with Czechoslovakia. The Wall fell on November 9, 1989. The world witnessed a flood of people resuming passage through the same Brandenburg Gate that had been sealed 10,316 days earlier. The Wall fell 27 days, less than one moon, after the 26th Spiral Calendar anniversary. The most remarkable event, the demonstration of 50,000 people standing up to an army, had occurred four days prior to that Spiral Calendar anniversary of August 12, 1961.

The fall of the Wall began speculation on the reunification of Germany. The standard wisdom of the time was that reunification would be a long process, if it could be done at all. The last time Germany had been ruled by one government of Germans was during World War II. This government ceased to operate upon the surrender to the Allies on May 7, 1945. The government was declared nonexistent on June 5, when the Allies proclaimed control of all operations in Germany. East Germany was not formed until 1949, when the West realized that the sector under Soviet control would not be allowed to merge with the sectors of Germany controlled by the Western Allies.

December 5, 1990 is the 28th Spiral Calendar anniversary of the German surrender. At this time, a divided Germany would have lasted 1.618 times as long as the Spiral Calendar length of the Berlin Wall. Germany, though, was no longer divided on December 5. The first elections to choose a government of unified Germany were held on December 3, 1990, just two days before the Spiral Calendar anniversary. Early planning had set December 3 for the reunification. Events moved fast and the actual reunification occurred on October 3, 1990. The speed at which reunification was effected surprised all the commentators, but when seen in a Spiral Calendar context, the events were a clockwork execution of a precise social pattern. Biological clocks determine the division of cells and the growth patterns of individual life. For Germany and the Berlin Wall, the Spiral Calendar determined the growth pattern of division and reunification of the societal life unit.

After freedom swept Eastern Europe, world attention shifted to the Soviet Union. A quick calculation shows that 1991 minus the 30th Spiral Calendar unit is 1917, the year of the Russian Revolution. My first calculation of an expected collapse of communism in the Soviet Union was for July 27 and 28, 1991. This was 26,937 days added to October 25 and 26 of 1917. Those are the dates listed in Leon Trotsky's *History of the Russian Revolution* as being the key turning point of the revolution. It was only later that I learned there was a different calendar in effect in Russia in 1917, known as "old style." The Trotsky dates converted to the Gregorian calendar are November 7 and 8, 1917. November 8 is when the Soviet Union celebrated the anniversary of the revolution. The name, October Revolution, is a holdover from the old style calendar. The night of November 7 and the morning of November 8 yielded the takeover of the winter palace in St. Petersburg. The 30th Spiral Calendar anniversary of the Russian revolution, calculated from November 8, 1917, was August 9, 1991, ten days before the coup of August 19, 1991. By August 22 of 1991, the coup had failed and the Bolsheviks irretrievably lost control of a government they had held for nearly 74 years. The number of moons during which the Bolsheviks ruled Russia is the square root of the 30th Fibonacci number plus *13 days*.

All of the Spiral Calendar relationships here display extraordinary precision, even when considering that political processes may seem less time oriented than financial ones. The years 1989-1991 contained a cluster of Spiral Calendar anniversaries of important communist institutions. None of those institutions survived one moon beyond the critical time period. The enabling condition for change in these political events was the people's loss of fear of their leaders. Fear is an emotion. It was an *emotional* change that characterized these dramatic social upheavals and made them similar to trend changes in financial markets.

The other pieces of the communist puzzle are China and Cuba. The same commentators who remark on the speed of the demise of European communism conversely ask how the Chinese regime withstood the Tianamen demonstrations of June 1989. The Peoples Republic of China was formed on October 1, 1949. There was no Spiral Calendar anniversary of this event in 1989. The next anniversary, $\sqrt{F_{28}}$ moons, of the formation of communist China is May 1, 1995. It would be ironic if the Chinese regime collapsed precisely on May Day, the important socialist holiday. The Chinese communists may survive until a later anniversary, such as September 2007 or July 2023.

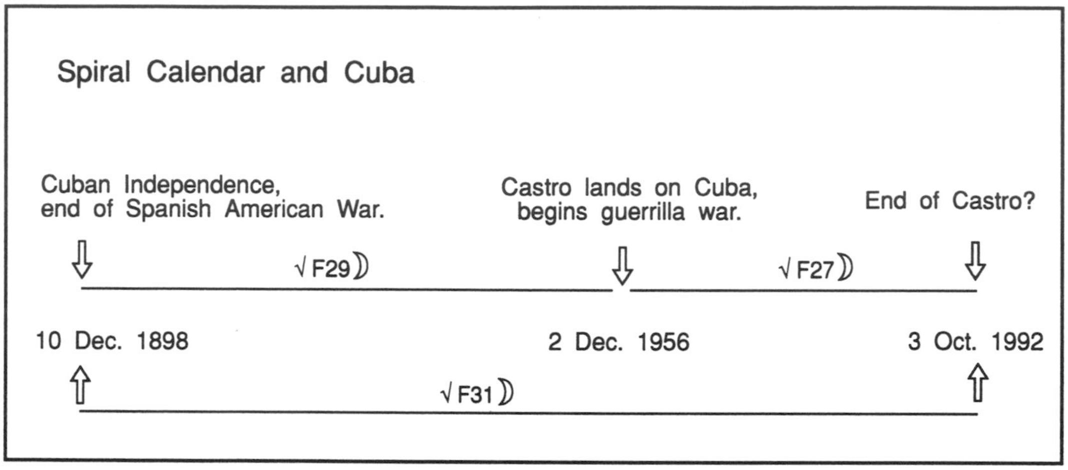

Spiral Calendar and Cuba

| Cuban Independence, end of Spanish American War. | | Castro lands on Cuba, begins guerrilla war. | | End of Castro? |

⇓   √ F29 ☽   ⇓   √ F27 ☽   ⇓

10 Dec. 1898   2 Dec. 1956   3 Oct. 1992

⇑   √ F31 ☽   ⇑

Figure 9-2

The Spiral Calendar relationships in Figure 9-1 all belong to the even additive sequence. An examination of the history of Cuba reveals a precise Spiral Calendar relationship on the odd additive sequence. Spain relinquished her sovereignty over Cuba at the end of the Spanish American war. The end of that war and the beginning of Cuban independence precisely date to December 10, 1898, when the Treaty of Paris was signed. American troops marched peacefully through Havana the following day, as the defeated Spanish army looked on. The next major conflict on Cuban soil began with the landing of Fidel Castro and Che Guevera's militia on the coast of Cuba. The date was December 2, 1956, exactly $\sqrt{F_{29}}$ moons from the end of the Spanish American war, *precise to the day*! See Figure 9-2. This began a two year guerrilla war, fought from the hills, which eventually toppled the Battista regime on January 1, 1959. (The Hungarian uprising also began on December 2, 1956. That revolt was crushed by Soviet tanks.)

Spiral Calendar anniversaries of both these events are due in the first week of October of 1992. As of this writing, the summer of 1992, the end of the Castro regime seems inevitable due to the loss of outside economic assistance from the former Soviet Union. At the present time, the press is not reporting any visible organized opposition to Castro in Cuba. Castro's regime may end within one moon of October 3, 1992, just as the Berlin Wall and the Soviet coup occurred within one moon of their respective Spiral Calendar anniversaries. If not, this time may see the beginning of the movement against him. Castro should lose power no later than November 1994, the Spiral Calendar anniversary of his accession.

THE HOSTAGES

When the hostage crisis wound down in December of 1991, news accounts showed the Cicippio family in front of a sign on their lawn that read; "Joseph Cicippio, free after 1908 days." I recognized that number and thought, "He was freed precisely on a Spiral Calendar anniversary of his capture." The hostage crisis was certainly one of the most emotional issues in American politics in the 1980s.

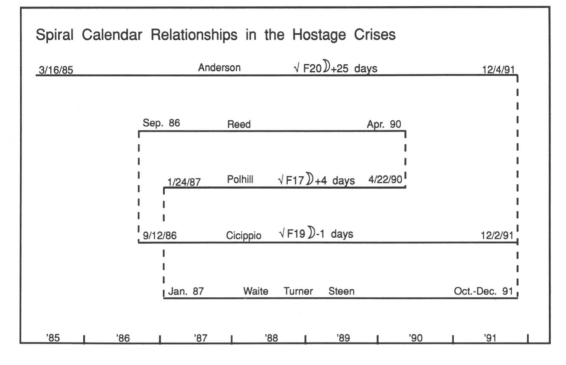

Figure 9-3

There were ten Americans captured and released by the terrorists. I will not consider the other Americans who escaped or were killed. Of the ten released, Terry Anderson was the longest held and the most visible in the media as a symbol of the crisis. The conclusion of the hostage crisis occurred with Mr. Anderson's release on December 4, 1991, 25 days after, and within one moon of, the 20th Spiral Calendar anniversary of his capture. The period from October to early December 1991 marked the dramatic final phase of the crisis, as four Americans and Britain's Terry Waite were released in the time span. The center of this crucial time frame, November 9, is the exact Spiral Calendar anniversary of Terry Anderson's capture.

Five of the Americans and Mr. Waite were captured in either September of 1986 or January of 1987. All of these men were released in the final phase of October-December or in April of 1990. Figure 9-3 shows how the two time periods of group captures and releases were Spiral Calendar units. From the September 1986 captures to the early

December 1991 releases was the 19th Spiral Calendar unit as represented by the release of Joseph Cicippio one day before the precise anniversary of his capture. The distance from the captures of January 1987 to the releases of April 1990 was the 17th Spiral Calendar unit. Robert Polhill was released four days after that anniversary of his capture. His time in captivity was .618 the length of Mr. Cicippio's. Not shown on the chart is the Rev. Lawrence Jenco. He was held for 564 days in 1985 and 1986, nine days short of a Spiral Calendar 573 days. Of the ten Americans, seven were released within one moon of a Spiral Calendar anniversary of their capture or the anniversary of another hostage's capture who was also released at that time.

The behavior of the captors was not far from the main subject matter of this book. They were traders, albeit in human flesh, and they were attempting to profit from their actions. For the hostages, their capture and release will represent the extreme low and high turning points on the charts of their lives.

There are so many events worldwide that cause us to stop and think, why did this happen now? To discover the larger patterns of the sequence of growth and decay, freedom and captivity and division and union is to begin to grasp the underlying purpose that is the process of life itself. Many events are impoverishing, injurious, hard and painful. When we can see the connection between these events and their positive and enriching counterparts across time, then we can begin to understand the condition of life. The contrast between perceived good and evil varies little from the contrast of spring and winter or full moon and new moon.

CHAPTER 10

FUTURE FORECASTS

Large spirals and other structures generate precise time windows resulting in precise forecasts. The magnitude of such spirals makes them portend the most important probable trend changes in the future. Examination of the degree, types of previous turns and the harmony, if any, involved will in most cases yield the degree and type of turn to expect.

One of the following forecasts is so far in the future that the majority of the traders who will experience this emotional event are not yet born. This forecast reflects the power of the Spiral Calendar and its reflection of the source of our emotions. I don't offer this forecast to be dramatic, but rather to make people aware of the larger trends that effect our lives.

Most forecasters are asked, "If your method works so well and many people begin using it, won't it stop working?" This is not a serious consideration. The forces that make people giddy at market tops and panicky at bottoms will not disappear just because we are conscious of them. I doubt that awareness of the Spiral Calendar will have a large scale effect on behavior. What if the answer to the question is yes? If people were to become large scale sellers into important tops and buyers at times of panics, the results would be beneficial. Foreknowledge would ameliorate the economic toll on society of emotional excesses in up and down markets. Society also stands to gain from a better understanding of the purpose of down cycles as part of the overall process of life. This involves an appreciation of the necessity for an economy to contract and rest in order to grow, not unlike a human's need to sleep in order to work.

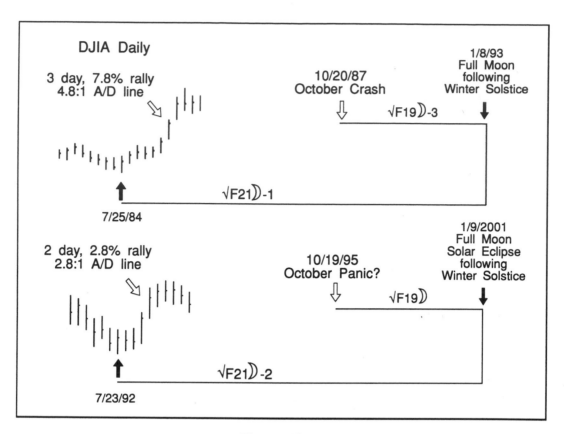

Figure 10-1

OCTOBER 1995

Perfect alternating spirals and October panics or massacres are ideal Spiral Calendar forecasting situations. If the July 1984 low, Figure 4-8, had been identified as the first point on a spiral back from the full moon following the winter solstice of January 1993, then the crash of 1987 could have been anticipated. Combine that spiral knowledge with the $\sqrt{F_{29}}$ relationship to 1929, and the forecasting advantage is tremendous. Figure 10-1 shows the similarities between the rally in late July 1984 and a similar occurrence in 1992. The 1992 rally was weaker and the low was penetrated within weeks. I believe this is because, unlike the 1984 example, it occurred within a larger bear market. See the section on October 1, 2004 that follows. Both lows preceding the rallies occurred on measurements backwards from full moons following winter solstices. If the 1992 example is the beginning of another spiral similar to Figure 4-8, then the next low will occur in October 1995. Additionally, October 1995 will be $\sqrt{F_{29}}$ from the slide of October 1937 (Figure 5-8), just as 1987 was $\sqrt{F_{29}}$ from 1929! Unlike 1937, 1995 *will* have the panic or massacre prerequisites, outlined in chapter 5, for an October top and bottom in the same month. A top $\sqrt{F_{16}}$ (2½ years) from the 1993 spring equinox new moon would fall near October 7, 1995, with the ideal bottom on October 19, 1995. A panic in 1995 should be smaller than 1987, just as the October 1937 drop was smaller than October 1929 and the 1992 rally in Figure 10-1 was smaller than the 1984 rally.

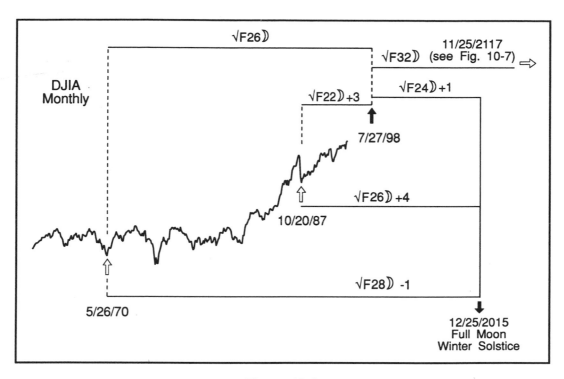

Figure 10-2

27 July 1998

Expect a major low in the Dow Jones Industrial Average near Monday, July 27, 1998. Figure 10-2 shows that this is the next occurrence of the full moon, winter equinox spiral shown in Figure 4-10. This great spiral first appeared in the 19th century with the "Silver Panic" of 1896. The last two occurrences of this spiral have been precise with large magnitude, the "Crash of 1987" and the low of May 1970. There is no reason to expect anything but a low for this date as it is associated with the full moon and the winter solstice, the negative forces. This is the only large magnitude precise turn in the decade of the 1990s that is likely to be a low. Any bear market that develops in the early to middle part of the decade will likely endure until this expected bottom. This is a valuable perspective that will avoid the decimation of capital for those who stay out of the bear's path.

An interesting sidelight to this spiral is that the full moon focus of December 25, 2015 measures $\sqrt{F}27+8$ days to the new moon, solar eclipse of February 16, 1980, which in turn followed the all time high in gold by 26 days (1 moon). The 27th Spiral Calendar unit is in harmony with the eclipse saros cycle. See Figure 4-18. The equivalent saros series eclipse near this focus is March 9, 2016.

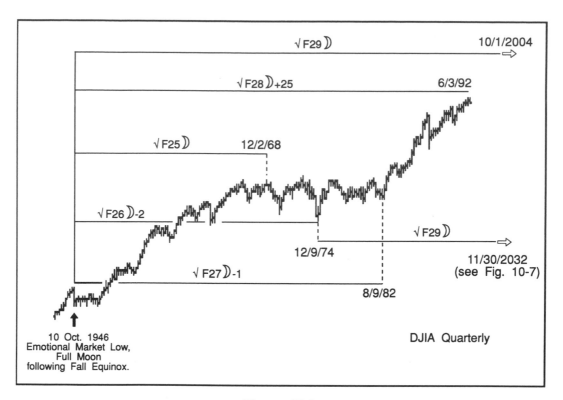

Figure 10-3

1 OCTOBER 2004

The large October 10, 1946 spiral, first presented in Figure 4-15, is updated in Figure 10-3. The all time high of the Dow Jones Industrial Average, as of this writing in August 1992, is June 3, 1992. This top is only 25 days after the next precise spiral calculation from October 1946 of Saturday, May 9, 1992. At first glance, this suggests only an approximate Spiral Calendar relationship. Charts of other markets, however, reveal that important market turns occurred on Monday, May 11. Figure 10-4 shows the Dow 65 Composite Average, in which the all time closing high is May 11, 1992. The Dow Composite includes the stocks of the Dow Transport and Utility Averages, as well as the Industrials. The Dow Industrial Average, when seen through the lens of another currency, the Japanese yen, topped precisely on May 11. The effect of May 11 was not limited to U.S. stocks. The London FT-SE 100 Index made its all time high on May 11, before dropping sharply in the ensuing 90 days. The importance of the spiral in Figure 10-3 and its confirmed arrival in the charts of Figure 10-4 allow the conclusion to be made that a bear market began on May 11, 1992, even though little time has passed or price drop has occurred in many averages at the time this book is going to press. Additionally, the stock markets of France, Germany, Mexico and Australia topped either near the May 11 London date or the June 3 Dow date. All these markets began sharp down turns in the summer of 1992.

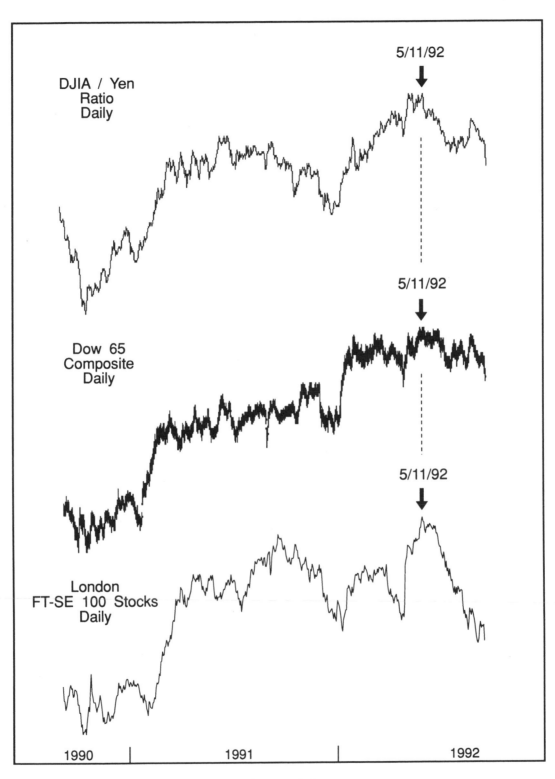

Figure 10-4

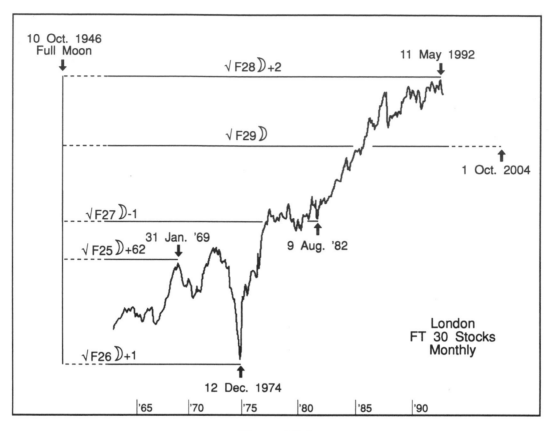

Figure 10-5

Figure 10-5 shows the long term relationships of this spiral for the London stock market. The FT 30 Index, which has a longer price history than the FT-SE 100, shares the precise turns of August 1982 and December 1974 with the Dow Industrials. The 1968-9 top was an approximate turn in London, much like May-June 1992 was approximate for the Dow Industrials.

The next occurrence within this spiral is October 1, 2004. This spiral has produced both tops (1968 and 1992) and bottoms (1974 and 1982). We do not have other spirals of this type (forward from full moon-fall equinox) to clue us whether to expect a high or low. The relationship to the focus will be $\sqrt{F}29$ moons, containing both solar and lunar harmonies. For this reason, there is the potential for an analogy to the sharp sell off of October 1946. In 2004, the full moon is due September 28, two days before the precise spiral calculation. The most likely occurrence at that time is for a market low.

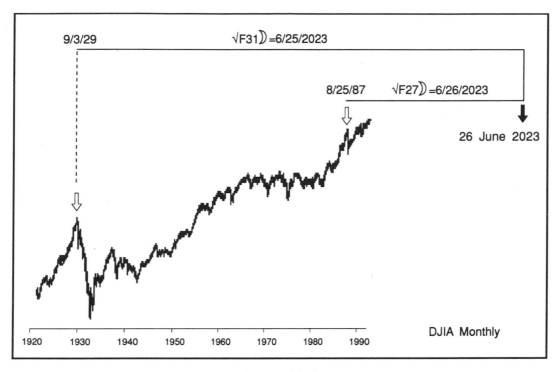

Figure 10-6

26 JUNE 2023

Monday, June 26, 2023 is the third point of a golden section including the 1929 and 1987 stock market tops in the United States, Figure 10-6. The golden section relationship to two important tops makes this expected turn a top. If we include the top of 1835 as part of the structure, implying a larger spiral, the focus is 16 or 17 of June 2081. This is near the summer solstice on the 20th. The summer solstice is a logical point for a focus of tops, as it is a positive force. The moon will be full on June 21, 2081, only sixteen hours after the solstice. There is no precedent for a full moon, summer solstice spiral that forms tops moving backwards. In any event, the great magnitude of the tops of 1835, 1929 and 1987 means that the potential of June 2023 is great for a market high.

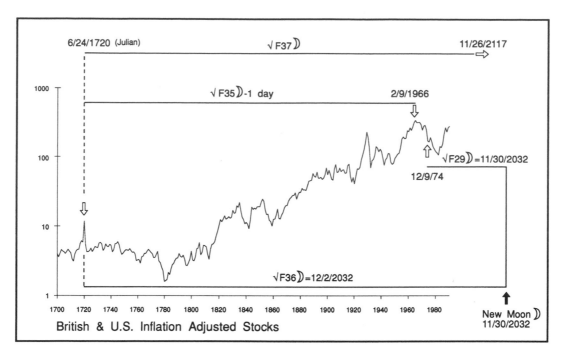

Figure 10-7

1 DECEMBER 2032

The largest known Spiral Calendar relationship is $\sqrt{F_{35}}$ moons from the South Sea Bubble of 1720 to the 20th century "real" stock price high of February 1966. If the 1966 top is the first point of a spiral whose focus is the bubble top, the next two points on that spiral are December 2, 2032 and November 26, 2117.

A forecast for a turn in December 2032 requires a precise measurement from two previous turns. Besides the focus, the 1966 top does not qualify, as the distance in time from 1966 to 2032 is not a Spiral Calendar period, but rather the difference between adjacent periods (see Appendix B.) Amazingly, there is another previous turn that measures to December 1, 2032, the U.S. stock market low of 1974. The bubble top of 1720 and the most important low to date in the second half of the 20th century both measure with one day precision to December 1, 2032. See Figure 10-7.

Figure 10-8 shows what we can expect in 2032 and why. The harmony of the periods leads me to expect a stock market low in a period of high inflation. Notice how 2032 contains lunar and solar harmony with 1974. In addition to the market low, 1974 saw a temporary spike in inflation before the larger inflationary top of 1980. The new moon is the positive force. There are new moons within days of all three points, 1720, 1974 and 2032. The positive force will be on inflation, not stocks. Which market will inflate? In 1974, grain prices made a major peak in October. The 1980 inflation was centered in gold and oil. An analogy to 1974

146

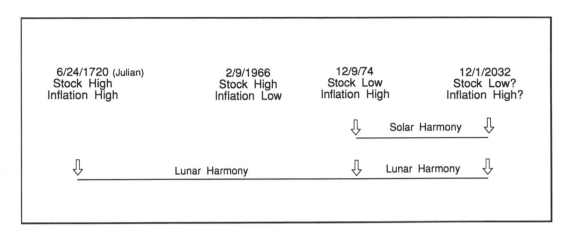

Figure 10-8

would look for a top in food prices in 2032. Keep in mind that the spiral structure here is much larger than 1974. An inflation in food in 2032 may resemble its focus, the full blown speculative mania of 1720, not just a bull market top. I am not alone in forecasting an inflation peak in 2032. A contemporary analyst has reached the same conclusion based on Kondratieff waves. Of course, this method does not pinpoint December 1 for the peak.

What characteristics should we expect of the stock market in 2032? The period from 1966 to 1974 saw the market move from a low inflation, high price climate to a high inflation, low price climate. A chart of nominal prices hides much of the price damage from inflation, unlike the chart of real, inflation adjusted prices. The forecast for the same type of turn in 2032, (low price, high inflation,) creates the possibility for the period of 1966 to 2032 to be a fractal, or larger scale, version of 1966 to 1974. This means that 1966 to 2032 will be a long sideways move in the market. This period will correct the two hundred years of bull market, which Figure 10-7 shows began in the late 18th century. This event will parallel 1966 to 1974, the shorter sideways move that digested the shorter bull market from the 1932 low.

The next point on the spiral from 1720, November 26, 2117, deserves mention here. Notice how it appears in both Figures 10-7 and 10-2. This date will be $\sqrt{F}37$ moons from 1720 and $\sqrt{F}33$ moons from 1966. It will also be $\sqrt{F}32$ moons from July 27, 1998, precise to one day. This future forecast will become a previous turn forecasting a turn on another spiral! Of the four structures in this chapter, two have precise relationships to a third. The 1946 and 2015 spirals have points that measure to the 1720 spiral, the largest magnitude spiral. 2032 measures from 1974 on the 1946 spiral and 1720. 2117 measures from 1998 on the 2015 spiral as well as 1720. See Figures 10-7 and 10-3. Other examples of interconnectivity are the nesting of spirals in Figures 4-7, 4-8, 4-10 and the linked relationships in Appendix B.

These large precise relationships are the ones I expect to be most reliable and critical to the U.S. stock market's path over the coming decades. Further research will undoubtedly reveal more structures, and the market's behavior over time may invalidate some existing structures. I do not doubt, however, that most of the examples of this chapter will mark extraordinary reversals of emotional market behavior.

CHAPTER 11

IS THE FUTURE PAST?

The Spiral Calendar raises intriguing questions in fields of study beyond markets. It also posits solutions to age old issues. The ideas that follow are intended to encourage debate.

FIBONACCI, TIME AND LIFE

Why is the Fibonacci sequence a characteristic of life? Why is the Spiral Calendar with its Fibonacci component the time piece of human growth and emotion? What is the nature of time, and how does it link with gravity in the life process?

First we must examine the nature of life. What distinguishes living things from non-living things? For non-living things to change, some action or energy must act on them. A rock may change when it is heated, dropped, or impacted by a larger rock. But when the rock is left alone, when it is in a stable environment, it will not change for an eternity. Living things are different. They will change, indeed must change, solely through the passage of time. A living thing, placed in a completely stable environment, will change without being acted upon by any force other than time. Time itself is part of the definition of life. As time passes, change occurs. Time is one of the ingredients of life. Change is a characteristic of life. Change cannot occur outside of time.

Einstein made great contributions to the understanding of time. His theories of relativity show how time and gravity are connected. The more gravity present, the slower time passes. Space and time are curved, and gravity is the force that bends, concluded Einstein. His work tells us that time does not flow. It exists much as space exists. There

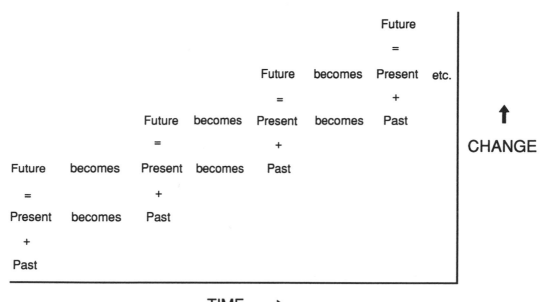

Figure 11-1

can be a place, now, where the past has not yet happened and another place can exist, also now, where the future has already occurred. This conflicts with our perception that time flows. It may be that our perception is different because we are of time and so do not readily perceive its real structure. Our position of being dependent upon time for our existence limits our ability to transcend time. We cannot see the forest because we are the trees. We cannot travel through time because we are "of time."

Time depends upon life, and Einstein's definition of time depends upon gravity. The properties of gravity give us clues to the nature of change in life through time. Paul Davies pinpoints gravity's unique relationship to time in his book, *The Cosmic Blueprint*: "Gravity pulls on every particle of matter in the universe and cannot be screened. Its effects are therefore cumulative and escalate with time." All other natural forces can be screened. An opaque object can screen light. Lead blocks radiation and insulation screens heat. Gravity is different. Because it cannot be screened, the gravity of yesterday must still be with us. The gravity of today is added to yesterday's to produce the gravity of the future. The past plus the present equals the future. This is the vertical axis in Figure 11-1. As time passes, the future becomes the present becomes the past. This is the horizontal axis reading across, in Figure 11-1. As time flows left to right, the cumulative nature of gravity produces change, bottom to top. This is why living things are not static. You cannot move across the time axis without moving up the change axis if you are subject to the cumulative properties of gravity-time, as life is.

The cumulative nature of gravity is a continuous additive process. If numbers are substituted for the words in Figure 11-1, using the numbers 1 and 1 for the first occurrence of past and present, the result is Figure 11-2. Here is the Fibonacci sequence

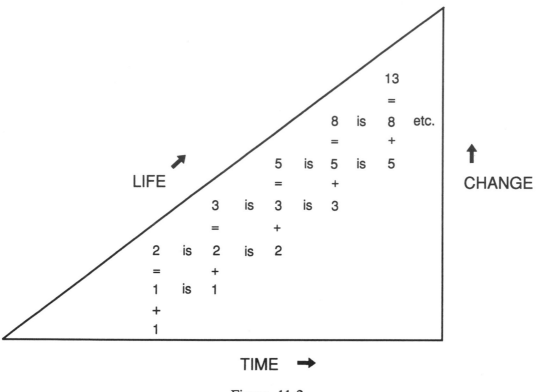

Figure 11-2

in all its beauty. The pattern is a triangle with sides labeled time and change and the resulting hypotenuse labeled life. Life exists at the point in the universe where gravity and time intersect. Gravity plus time equals life.

We met this equation in Chapter 3, $\phi + \phi^2 = \phi \times \phi^2$. Phi is the location in the universe of numbers where a number added to its square equals the number multiplied by its square. This meeting of addition and multiplication explains the relationship between gravity, life and time. As time passes, gravity adds, and as gravity adds, life multiplies. It has long been known that ϕ is ubiquitous in life forms. Now it can be understood why. Gravity is a continuous additive process, and wherever additive processes exist, ϕ is present. The additive nature of life is evident in the procreative process. Our parents add together to produce us. One plus one equals two, plus one equals three, Fibonacci. We are produced from those in the past. We are the sum of our parents each of whom is the sum of his/her parents.

The Spiral Calendar adds to the examples of Fibonacci in nature with evidence of the Fibonacci sequence in the emotional behavior of man across the dimension of time in units of a gravitational pulse, the lunar phase.

WHY?

The gravity of the Earth pulls down. The gravity of the sun and the moon pulls up. The life process strives towards the source of the energy that creates and sustains. Consider the allusions to life in our language. We grow "up," then as age sets in we "succumb to gravity." Think of a lifeless earth as a smooth cueball and an earth with life as a peach covered with fuzz. The fuzz are the life forms pulled from the earth by the gravitational forces of the sun-moon rhythm. I believe that if there was no moon, there would be no life on Earth. What would life be like if there was more than one moon?

Time defines life, and the seasons define time. So much of life is controlled by the seasons. This book describes life in terms of the lunar and spiral seasons, not just the obvious solar seasons. Notice how the forms of life differ greatly over time, so-called evolution. While it is often asked why the dinosaurs became extinct, the question might be asked, why is life not evolving *into* dinosaurs now? If we look at gravity as accumulating, then we understand that the quantity of this accumulation now should be much greater than at any previous time in history. This may explain the increasing complexity of life forms as time progresses.

The equation that produces the lunar-solar rhythm is also changing over time. The moon is very gradually moving away from the earth. This fact implies that the gravitational life force was stronger in the past than the present. The size of life forms that can be created may relate to the quantity of the gravitational pulse of the sun and moon. The size of dinosaurs may be impossible to achieve on earth now due to the weakening of the gravitational pull up as the moon recedes from the earth.

The Spiral Calendar raises further questions about evolution. The theory of evolution has never explained why life does not evolve gradually over time. Fossil records indicate that life forms are stable over long periods of time before changing dramatically in a short period of time. This fact definitely lies beyond the bounds of natural selection. The Spiral Calendar shows how there can be certain time periods in which life forms make dramatic changes in their direction of development. The change in Russian society on the Spiral Calendar anniversary of the 1917 revolution discussed in Chapter 9 is an example.

INDIVIDUAL BEHAVIOR PRODUCES GROUP ORDER

How does the behavior of individuals, when viewed as a group in the pattern of stock prices, contain an orderly structure with implications of a predetermined path? There is a conflict between what we perceive of our freedom and individuality of action and the spiral patterns set forth in this book, which display an order encompassing millions of people spanning generations and centuries. Common sense tells us that orderly patterns are produced by many working together in a structured situation, not by individuals free to act as they desire. The facts do not bear this out.

There is a parallel to this apparent conflict in the laws of physics, as they have become to be understood in the twentieth century. The classic Newtonian view of the world was that the physical world could be understood as the laws governing matter became known. Einstein added new twists with his theories of relativity. Time could move at different speeds and space-time could be curved by gravity. But these were still laws, nonetheless and they described a world that was predictable, although Einstein's version was certainly less comprehensible. Physics was driven to find not only every law governing the physical world, but also to explore the physical world in smaller and smaller scales, from molecules to atoms and then to subatomic particles. The discovery of quantum mechanics permanently jarred the notion of predictability.

Quantum mechanics is the study of what occurs at the atomic level. Quantum theory holds that the behavior of atoms and subatomic particles is truly random. The mechanical laws of physics say that if you know the location of an object and its momentum, you can then calculate where it's going. It is predictable. In the quantum world, you cannot know where a particle is *and* what its momentum is. You can know one or the other piece of information, but not both. The behavior of the subatomic particle is therefore unpredictable, random. Quantum theory has been proven in scientific experiments and is accepted by the scientific community. Its discovery has led directly to lasers, transistors and nuclear power.

The idea that the smallest particles are truly random has bred the conclusion that all of the physical universe must be random. This is not a conclusion of quantum mechanics, but an outgrowth of the process of its discovery, the search to understand the sequentially smaller levels of matter. The original motivating thought was that if order were found at the minutest degree, then the ordering forces at all levels would be understood. When the world at the atomic level was found to be random, the conclusion by philosophers was drawn, wrongly I believe, that the entire universe is random. The result was existentialism and nihilism. These ideas became fashionable in the 1920s, the same period as the discovery of quantum mechanics.

The ability of atomic particles, with their characteristics of individuality, to behave as an ordered structure when grouped at the molecular level serves as an example to help us understand how humans can pursue their individual agendas and yet, without intention, produce a larger ordered structure. In fact ultimately, when viewed as a societal whole, human actions assume the shapes, structures and fractal patterns found elsewhere throughout nature.

The perception of order in human life is inspired by the large amount of order and beauty in the plant and animal kingdom. The magnificent patterns and abilities of nature project a structure to all life on earth. The contrast is the anarchy and destruction of which man and nature are each capable. These tendencies are the evidence for the believers in randomness. The order of the Spiral Calendar possesses the beauty, precision and structure common to all of nature's life forms. Through this mechanism, man can see how the individual's behavior coalesces to build the patterns of life just as the birds, turtles, lemmings, bees, ants and other creatures display mass organization and pattern in their community endeavors.

The irony is that, among humans, those who argue that life is random and without structure use that argument to impose rules and laws on men, depriving them of their individuality and free will. Those societies that possess artificial orders invariably fail in building the economic systems required to provide for their communities, witness communism. It is a higher level of understanding to realize that individual freedom is a prerequisite for the natural order to emerge. Our desire for an imposed order is always inversely proportional to the quantity of natural order perceived around us. The less order we sense in the world, the more some people desire to impose on themselves and others.

The final realization that the Spiral Calendar makes clear is that our whole being and existence are part *of* nature, not foreign and alien *to* nature. The pattern of perfect spirals containing market lows are no different from the patterns of the seasons across time, the Nautilus shell, a spider's web or any other of nature's wonders.

APPENDIX A

SPIRAL CALENDAR

Here are the first thirty-nine units of the Spiral Calendar in an expanded listing. The calendar is denominated in both natural and manmade time units. The conversions into manmade time units are provided for comparative purposes with known cycle frequencies and other timing methods. I believe there is no intrinsic numerologic value to specific manmade time units. The Spiral Calendar life force predates the origin of the modern month (by two thousand years) and the modern week (by three thousand years.)

The expanded calendar also lists the difference of adjacent Spiral Calendar units as a sequence, $F_{(n+1)} - F_n$. These are denominated in days and years. This sequence is helpful for finding large Spiral Calendar relationships with limited data. Clusters generated solely by this sequence seem to be unreliable, but they can provide clues to the presence of larger spirals.

Fibonacci		Natural Time			Man Made Time		$\sqrt{F_{(n+1)}}-\sqrt{F_n}$	
n	F_n	Moons	Days	Years	Weeks	Months	Days	Years
1	1	1.00	29.5	.1	4.2	1.0		
2	1	1.00	29.5	.1	4.2	1.0	12.2	
3	2	1.41	41.8	.1	6.0	1.4	9.4	
4	3	1.73	51.1	.1	7.3	1.7	14.9	
5	5	2.24	66.0	.2	9.4	2.2	17.5	
6	8	2.83	83.5	.2	11.9	2.7	22.9	.1
7	13	3.61	106.5	.3	15.2	3.5	28.8	.1
8	21	4.58	135.3	.4	19.3	4.4	36.9	.1
9	34	5.83	172.2	.5	24.6	5.7	46.8	.1
10	55	7.42	219.0	.6	31.3	7.2	59.6	.2
11	89	9.43	278.6	.8	39.8	9.2	75.8	.2
12	144	12.00	354.4	1	50.6	11.6	96.4	.3
13	233	15.26	450.8	1.2	64.4	14.8	122.6	.3
14	377	19.42	573.4	1.6	81.9	18.8	156.0	.4
15	610	24.70	729.4	2.0	104.2	24.0	198.4	.5
16	987	31.42	927.7	2.5	132.5	30.5	252.4	.7
17	1597	39.96	1180.1	3.2	168.6	38.8	321.0	.9
18	2584	50.83	1501.1	4.1	214.4	49.3	408.3	1.1
19	4181	64.66	1909.5	5.2	272.8	62.7	519.4	1.4
20	6765	82.25	2428.9	6.6	347.0	79.8	660.7	1.8
21	10946	104.62	3089.6	8.5	441.4	101.5	840.4	2.3
22	17711	133.08	3930.0	10.8	561.4	129.1	1069.0	2.9
23	28657	169.28	4999.1	13.7	714.2	164.2	1359.8	3.7
24	46368	215.33	6358.9	17.4	908.4	208.9	1729.7	4.7
25	75025	273.91	8088.6	22.1	1155.5	265.7	2200.3	6.0
26	121393	348.41	10288.9	28.2	1469.8	338.0	2798.8	7.7
27	196418	443.19	13087.7	35.8	1869.7	430.0	3560.1	9.7
28	317811	563.75	16647.8	45.6	2378.3	547.0	4528.3	12.4
29	514229	717.10	21176.3	58.0	3025.2	695.7	5760.3	15.8
30	832040	912.16	26936.7	73.7	3848.1	885.0	7327.3	20.1
31	1346269	1160.29	34264.0	93.8	4894.9	1125.7	9320.5	25.5
32	2178309	1475.91	43584.5	119.3	6226.4	1431.9	11855.8	32.5
33	3524578	1877.39	55440.3	151.8	7920.0	1821.4	15080.9	41.3
34	5702887	2388.07	70521.2	193.1	10074.5	2316.9	19183.1	52.5
35	9227465	3037.67	89704.3	245.6	12814.8	2947.2	24401.3	66.8
36	14930352	3863.98	114105.7	312.4	16300.8	3748.9	31039.0	85.0
37	24157817	4915.06	145144.7	397.4	20735.0	4768.6	39482.2	108.1
38	39088169	6252.05	184626.9	505.5	26375.3	6065.8	50222.1	137.5
39	63245986	7952.73	234849.0	643.0	33549.9	7715.8	63883.5	174.9

APPENDIX B

THE 19TH CENTURY

The chart for Appendix B depicts the known Spiral Calendar relationships of the nineteenth century. Most of the relationships in the chart are precise to within one moon. The only problematical measurement is the exact timing of the top of 1835, which was discusssed in Chapter 4. The well documented boom/bust cycles of the 19th century and the frequent panics of the era yield an extraordinary web of Spiral Calendar relationships.

The panic on the continent in 1799 and the major speculative top of 1835 are related by $\sqrt{F_{28}}$ moons. In turn, these two points are foci that link the panics and/or tops of 1857, 1873 and 1893. Notice the interlocking nature of the relationships. Only the panics of 1819, 1884 and 1896 do not figure in this large structure. The latter two panics were the first two points in important twentieth century spirals.

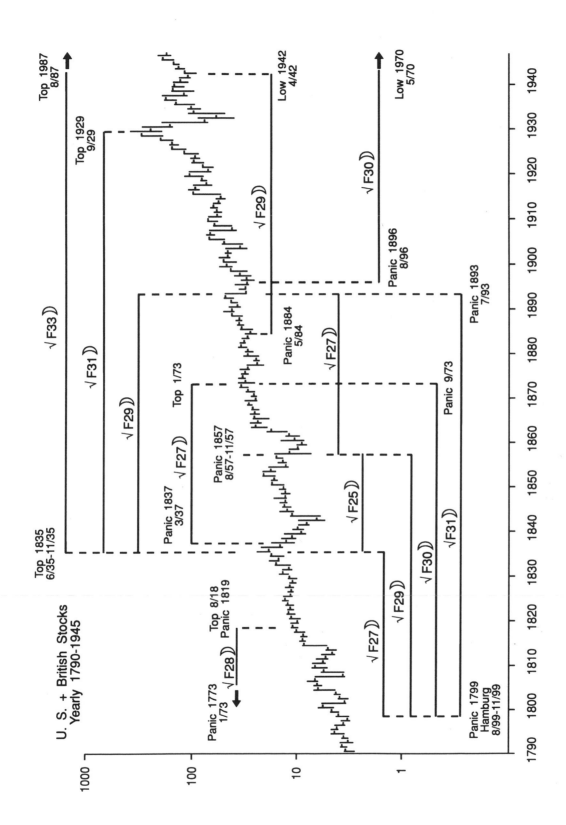

BIBLIOGRAPHY

Cain, Kathleen. *Luna: Myth and Mystery*. Johnson Books. Boulder. 1991.

Cook, Theodore. *The Curves of Life*. Dover. New York. 1979

Cotterell, Arthur. *A Dictionary of World Mythology*. Oxford Press. Oxford. 1986

Davies, Paul. *The Cosmic Blueprint*. Simon and Schuster. New York. 1988.

Doczi, Georgy. *The Power of Limits*. Shambhala. Boston. 1981.

Frost and Prechter. *Elliott Wave Principle*. New Classics Library. Gainesville. 1978.

Ghyka, Matila. *The Geometry of Art and Life*. Dover. NewYork. 1977.

Hambidge, Jay. *The Elements of Dynamic Symmetry*. Dover. New York. 1967.

Huntley, H.E. *The Divine Proportion*. Dover. New York. 1970.

Katzeff, Paul. *Moon Madness*. Citadel Press. Secaucus. 1981.

Kindleberger, Charles P. *Manias, Panics and Crashes*. Basic Books. 1989.

Langdon, S. *Babylonian Menologies and the Semitic Calendars*. Kraus Reprint. 1980.

Lawlor, Robert. *Sacred Geometry*. Crossroad. New York. 1982.

Leiber, Arnold L. *The Lunar Effect*. Anchor Press/Doubleday. New York. 1978.

Long, Kim. *The Moon Book*. Johnson Books. Boulder. 1988.

Mackay, Charles. *Extraordinary Popular Delusions and the Madness of Crowds*. London. 1841.

Oates, Joan. *Babylon*. Thames and Hudson. London. 1979.

Oppenheim, A. Leo. *Ancient Mesopotamia*. Univ. of Chicago Press. Chicago. 1964.

Ottewell, Guy. *The Under-Standing of Eclipses*. Astronomical Workshop. Greenville. 1991.

Prechter, R., ed. *The Major Works of R.N. Elliott*. New Classics Library. Gainesville. 1980.

Sobel, Robert. *Panic on Wall Street*. Dutton. New York. rev. 1988.

Thompson, D'Arcy. *On Growth and Form*. Cambridge Univ. Press. Cambridge. 1917.

Tompkins, Peter. *Secrets of the Great Pyramid*. Harper and Row. New York. 1971.

Wall, Alban. *Stonehenge and the Calendar of Coligny*. Epigraphic Society Publications. 1989.

White, Eugene ed. *Crashes and Panics*. Dow Jones-Irwin. 1990.

Other Titles From New Classics Library

Elliott Wave Principle - Key to Stock Market Profits
A.J. Frost and Robert R. Prechter, Jr.

The Major Works of R.N. Elliott
Robert R. Prechter, Jr., ed.

A Turn in the Tidal Wave
Robert R. Prechter, Jr.

Popular Culture and the Stock Market - A Collection, 1983-1991
Robert R. Prechter, Jr.

Fibonacci Numbers
N. Vorobev

Leonard of Pisa and the New Mathematics of the Middle Ages
Joseph and Frances Gies

R. N. Elliott's Market Letters, 1938-1945
Robert R. Prechter Jr., ed.

Coming Soon:

The Complete Elliott Wave Writings of Hamilton Bolton
Robert R. Prechter Jr., ed.

CAROLAN'S
Spiral Calendar™
Research

Christopher Carolan, Editor   Vol. 1 #1

INVESTORS-TRADERS:
NEXT SPIRAL TURN DUE!

Would you like precise forecasts for the next emotional extremes, "lunacy," in market behavior?

If you're an investor or trader, *Carolan's Spiral Calendar Research* (CSCR) is a great new source of low-risk investment opportunities. Every month Christopher Carolan combines Spiral Calendar™ analysis with sentiment measures of the market's emotional health to analyze U.S. stocks and bonds, precious metals and selected foreign stock markets.

Mr. Carolan's easy-to-read commentary is shaped by his seven years as a professional floor trader. He traded in a "pit," the emo-tional nerve center of today's markets. *CSCR* will bring you the same visionary and creative market forecasts that made his book, *The Spiral Calendar*, a groundbreaking work.

As a subscriber, you can be among the first to invest by using the latest advances in Mr. Carolan's research. He'll use past results and forecasts to provide long, intermediate and short-term market analysis. *Interim Bulletins* supplement the twelve regular issues to bring you the best opportunities in today's markets.

Fill out, cut or copy, then mail the coupon below, or call (404) 531-3060 for more information. Don't miss the next spiral turn!

☐ *CAROLAN'S* Spiral Calendar Research - 1 year subscription... $279.00*

☐ *CAROLAN'S* Spiral Calendar Research - 3 issue trial.. $75.00

☐ *The Spiral Calendar* - Book... $84.00**

send to Calendar Research, Inc. Distribution Center P.O. Box 41 Gainesville GA 30503 phone orders call 404-531-3060	pro-rata refunds *guaranteed* sub-total _____ Shipping and handling: GA residents add appropriate sales tax _____ * overseas add $20.00 ** North America add $5.00 Shipping and handling_____ ** overseas add $16.00 Total _____ ☐ check enclosed, U.S. funds only, or charge my ☐ VISA ☐ MC #_____ exp. date _____

Spiral Calendar™ is a trademark of Calendar Research, Inc.